GOURMET INDIAN

IN MINUTES

OVER 140 INNOVATIVE RECIPES

GOURMET INDIAN
IN MINUTES

MONISHA BHARADWAJ

WITH PHOTOGRAPHS BY GUS FILGATE

Kyle Books

DEDICATION

This book is especially for my son, Arrush, who is passionate about food, and for my daughter, Saayli, who finds it impossible to be interested in it at all. I am inspired to innovate by both—either to please one palate or to tempt the other.

Design Mark Latter at Vivid Design
Editor Stephanie Horner
Photography by Gus Filgate
Home economy by Annie Nicholls
Printed by Star Standard, Singapore

Monisha Bharadwaj is hereby identified as the author of this work in accordance with Section 77 of the Copyright, Designs, and Patents Act 1988.

2 4 6 8 10 9 7 5 3 1

ISBN 978 1 904920 73 1

This edition published in 2008 by Kyle Books
An imprint of Kyle Cathie Limited
www.kylecathie.com

Distributed by National Book Network
4501 Forbes Blvd., Suite 200
Lanham, MD 20706
Phone: (301) 459 3366 Fax: (301) 429 5746

First published in Great Britain in 2002 by Kyle Cathie Limited as *Stylish Indian in Minutes*

Printed and bound in Singapore by Star Standard

CONTENTS

INTRODUCTION

I set up my first home in England when I was twenty-two years old. I had arrived from Bombay and from a household where servants did the shopping, cooking, and cleaning. I had never bought or checked groceries and had certainly not cooked on a daily basis. As a graduate of hotel management, my time in my mother's kitchen had been spent whipping up exotic international delicacies such as Poulet Marengo and Tarte Rustique aux Abricots, much to the delight of my family and friends, who would devour my offerings with utmost enthusiasm and relish.

My first few days in England were an eye-opener. There were endless calls to Bombay asking for home recipes and measures. "Which rice do I use?" or "Oh no! I can't get fresh coconut here," and then, "Even if I find one, how do I grate it?"

With time, I have learned that every cook finds a balance of her or his own. As my work and study pressures began to build, I found that I craved home food more and more. I bought several books on Indian cooking but found, to my dismay, that they made Indian food out to be an "exotic" cuisine that was only good after hours of soaking, grinding, and cooking. I neither had the time nor the inclination to get into these tedious procedures.

My mother had been a busy, successful working woman all her life, and I knew that every time she cooked, for parties or festivals, she was able to create miracles in minutes. I began devising my own techniques and tricks. I wanted authentic Indian food, was not willing to compromise on taste or quality, and I wanted it on my table in minutes rather than hours. By this time, I was also entertaining a lot, and guess what my friends always asked for? Home-cooked Indian food! I soon found that time is inversely proportionate to innovation, and I tried out countless recipes using endless variations until I taught myself a style that I was comfortable with.

Needless to say, I'm not the only one who has pared down the fuss and bother of Indian festive cooking. I say "festive," meaning special or celebratory, whether a meal for two or a gathering of fifty, because Indian home cooking has always been relatively straightforward. Today's young homemakers in India are just as keen to find ways to reduce time in the kitchen, using the hours saved to pursue a career, a hobby, or to be with the family.

WHAT IS STYLISH INDIAN?

In order to save time and effort, one cannot just put together anything. I strongly believe that a cook must respect authenticity, be committed to nutrition and taste, and enjoy presenting food beautifully. Food has to look "good enough to eat" and must fulfill all nutritional requirements. All too often Indian food outside India has simply

meant a "curry." The cuisines of the many states of India, regional variations, innovations, and evolved recipes find no place in the Indian restaurants around the world. In this book, I have put together a collection of recipes that are suited to the modern busy lifestyle and yet are festive and special. All the recipes, some classic, others new, reflect an evolving Indian cuisine that is truer to today's needs.

INGREDIENTS

My experience has taught me to buy the most dewy, most crisp, and most fragrant fruits and vegetables for my kitchen. My meat, poultry, fish, and eggs must be the freshest available or I will not buy. I look for prime cuts bursting with goodness. In selecting spices I look for fat, perfumed pods that will create mystery and allure in my cooking. Milk and milk products must be positively straight off the farm. There are a few concessions: I use store-bought spices and I am thankful for treasures such as canned beans, tamarind paste, and tomato paste.

There is an endless variety of Indian breads, some of which can be bought. These would typically include nans, rotis (also called chapatis), parathas, with or without herbs, and pita bread. I would say that one should eat store-bought breads within two days, but as they freeze well, they can be kept in the freezer for about one week.

A word on chilies: I don't often seed the less hot green chilies since their seeds are not easy to remove. If you don't like your food too hot, just reduce the number of chilies. However, it's slightly different with the red varieties, such as the Kashmiri, which are often in the dish as much to provide color as heat. If you want to reduce the level of heat without compromising on the color, I would suggest you do remove their seeds.

A point worth noting is that if you have eaten something containing more chili than you can bear, reach for your yogurt-based raita. The capsaicin in chilies is responsible for their heat, and it's insoluble in water or beer, so neither can help you recover! Yogurt, on the other hand, neutralizes capsaicin and is most effective at cooling your tongue.

TECHNIQUES

I use my free time to preprepare some ingredients to speed up recipes later:

❖ For ginger-garlic paste, I often buy premade pastes and combine them in a ratio of one to one so that I just need one spoon and one bottle. Most Indian recipes call for a bit of both anyway.
❖ Roasted ground cumin is a wonderful spice to have in your cupboard, since it gives a lift to almost any savory dish. Simply heat a dry pan and drop in a few tablespoons of cumin seeds. Stir them until they become dark. Grind them to a powder in a coffee grinder or a small blender and store in a dry jar.
❖ Many of the recipes involve frying masala pastes and spice powders. Always cook these on a very low heat, or they will burn. A blended spice paste is cooked when the mixture starts to separate from the cooking oil.

My pantry ingredients:
❖ cans of beans: red kidney, flageolets, lima beans, chickpeas, cannellini
❖ cans of pineapple
❖ cans of tomatoes—whole peeled plum, chopped, puréed
❖ cans of evaporated milk, cream, coconut milk, and lentil soup
❖ many kinds of nuts: almonds, pistachios, peanuts, mixed nuts, cashews, pine nuts, ground almonds
❖ jars of mint sauce (great stirred into yogurt as a dip with kabobs, samosas, and bhajias) and apple sauce (to go with fritters)
❖ a few kinds of salt—coarse or kosher, garlic, onion, sea
❖ olive oil infused with garlic or lemon for an instant salad dressing
❖ whole-grain mustard, peanut butter
❖ tamarind paste, dried coconut, pickled green peppers
❖ granulated sugar, brown cane sugar
❖ spices and mixtures—garam masala, tandoori masala, cardamom pods, and cumin seeds (far better to buy the cardamom pods and grind your own powder as you need it)
❖ honey

EQUIPMENT

You don't need any special utensils or cooking pots other than a few different sized, good-quality, heavy, lidded pans or casserole dishes. The type that can be used on the stovetop and then be transferred directly to the oven is most useful, especially as you can begin by frying onions, garlic, spices, and pastes in them, then add meat, vegetables, lentils, and liquid, and bring to a boil—an all-in-one large pot. Indian cooks will have at least one pressure cooker, which suits this sequence of intense cooking processes perfectly. Many in the West consider the pressure cooker an old-fashioned device, but I find it indispensable, and the dish is cooked in no time at all. If you don't have any all-purpose casserole dishes or a pressure cooker, select a large frying pan for the initial frying or browning, then transfer everything to a saucepan or an ovenproof casserole dish. Do read each recipe carefully to check that the pan you select is large enough to take all the ingredients and the liquid.

In India we use woks, or *kadhai*, in a similar way to the Chinese, for stir-frying and deep-frying. The *kadhai*, made of aluminum, is heavier than a Chinese wok, as it is has to be used over the heat for longer periods without the food burning.

You will need a grinder of some sort. There are powerful electric blenders that can grind dry and wet ingredients to make powders or pastes. For small quantities, a coffee grinder is a good way to grind spices. Dry-roasted seeds become brittle and can be effectively ground in a mortar in the time-honored fashion. But an all-purpose food processor that can grate, chop, and knead is becoming increasingly popular in Indian kitchens.

MEASURES

This book is a reflection of my own experience as well as that of many Indians who have now moved toward a way of cooking that is easy and involves a minimum of fuss. There is no set way of cooking in India, and my methods often don't give an exact cooking time. I would ask that you use your judgment, eyes, and taste frequently. This is, after all, how to cook properly and to gain personal experience and confidence. I hope that this book will inspire my readers to experiment with ingredients and come up with innovative and delicious meals like many modern Indian people do today. The book is for all of us who would like to spend less time in the making of Indian food and more in its enjoyment.

With the exception of the Indian-Style Fried Eggs (page 115) and Fruit Ice Candy Sticks (page 140), all recipes are for four servings.

TRADITIONAL INDIAN COOKING DOES NOT BOAST A GREAT SOUP AND APPETIZER REPERTOIRE. IN FACT, APPETIZERS ARE OFTEN FOUND AT "WESTERNIZED" INDIAN RESTAURANTS RATHER THAN IN HOMES, EXCEPT ON SPECIAL OCCASIONS. An Indian meal has all courses served simultaneously, including the dessert. I like to serve soup at dinner parties simply because it is a way of gently enticing the tastebuds and preparing them for the meal to come.

My chapter on soups and appetizers has recipes from homes where appetizers are served or from colder northern India, where, as in the West, the climate dictates the necessity of a warming broth. The meat-based cooking of northern Indians has delicately flavored consommés and stocks, served on special occasions, and *shorbas* or cream soups, thickened with flour, smoothed with cream, and eaten with rice. The Raj left a legacy of Anglo-Indian food, including Mulligatawny, meaning "pepper water" *(molaga + tanni)* in Tamil, the language of southern India, where this soup originated. In the south, a spicy *rasam* or thin, highly spiced lentil broth is sometimes served as a soup. In the scorching summer, cool yogurt-based soups are preferred.

SOUPS
AND
APPETIZERS

A delicacy from Karnataka on India's west coast, this tangy soup can be served hot or cold. It is sometimes made without the coconut milk for a thinner soup, with a few curry leaves for flavor. It is also eaten mixed with rice. Choose the reddest tomatoes you can find for the best color.

TOMATOCHE SAAR

spicy tomato soup

Preparation time: 5 minutes

Cooking time: 15 minutes

1. Make a shallow cross on the bottom of each tomato using a sharp knife. Place them in a pot, along with the chili, peppercorns, cumin seeds, and salt, and just cover with boiling water.

2. When the tomatoes become mushy (this takes about 5 minutes), lift out with a slotted spoon and peel off the skin. Return the flesh to the water. Cool slightly.

3. Whiz the mixture in a blender. Add the coconut milk and adjust seasoning.

4. Heat gently and serve garnished with a sprig of cilantro.

2 large, fresh tomatoes (about 10 ounces)

1 green chili

6 peppercorns

½ teaspoon cumin seeds

Water to cover

Salt, to taste

1¼ cups canned coconut milk

Cilantro sprigs, for garnish

*This soup comes from Rajasthan, where the intense sun creates multicolored mirages.
In the dry, tropical heat, this soup is like ambrosia from the heavens. Best served in a
flower-filled summer garden to refresh your guests on a hot summer's day!*

KHEERE KA THANDA SHORBA

chilled summer cucumber soup

1. Whiz the cucumber in a blender, then stir in the yogurt and garlic.

2. Strain through a fine-mesh strainer, making sure you squeeze out all the cucumber juice.

3. Whisk in enough water to make up to 2½ cups. Chill. Season with salt and pepper just before serving.

4. Serve garnished with mint and float an ice cube on top.

Preparation time: 15 minutes

1 English cucumber, peeled

1¼ cups plain yogurt

1 clove of garlic, crushed

Salt and freshly ground black pepper, to taste

1 teaspoon fresh mint, finely chopped, or mint leaves, for garnish

Saffron is considered the spice of the gods because it is so fragile and pure. Its inclusion in any recipe assures sophistication and celebration. This aromatic and colorful soup adds flair to an Indian meal. It can be made quickly and, as a real treat, garnished with a piece of edible silver foil (varq), available from most Indian grocery stores.

KESARI MURGH KA SHORBA

chicken and saffron soup

1. Heat the oil in a large, heavy pot and add the cumin seeds.

2. As the seeds darken, add the cubed chicken and peppercorns and stir until the chicken turns opaque.

3. Add the stock and salt, and bring to a boil.

4. Reduce heat and simmer until the chicken is cooked.

5. To serve, shred the chicken into the bottom of warmed individual bowls and pour in the soup. Sprinkle a pinch of saffron strands over each one (the soup should turn a delicate orange). Serve hot.

1 teaspoon sunflower oil

½ teaspoon cumin seeds

2 cups cubed, boneless chicken

½ teaspoon crushed peppercorns

3 cups chicken stock

Salt, to taste

¼ teaspoon saffron strands

Preparation time: 10 minutes   Cooking time: 15 minutes

PANEER BHARE AVOCADO

avocado filled with cottage cheese

Preparation time: 10 minutes

1. Cut to the middle of the avocados from the stalk end, easing around the pit. Twist both halves carefully and lift apart. Remove pit. Brush the surface with lemon juice to prevent discoloration.

2. Fill each avocado half with the pineapple cottage cheese, and chill.

3. To serve, sprinkle with coarse salt, roasted ground cumin, and chili powder. Place each avocado half on a mixture of red and green lettuce leaves.

2 large avocados
1 teaspoon lemon juice
⅔ cup cottage cheese with pineapple
Coarse salt or kosher, for sprinkling
¼ teaspoon roasted ground cumin
Pinch of chili powder
Mixed lettuce leaves, for serving

CHEESE AUR MIRCH KA TOAST

chili cheese toast

Preparation time: 5 minutes
Cooking time: 5 minutes

1. Lightly mix the cheese and the chili.

2. Toast the bread and spread with butter. Divide the cheese mixture between the four slices and spread to cover. Season with salt and pepper. Place under a hot broiler until the cheese begins to melt and turns golden brown.

3. Cut each slice into four triangles and serve with curly lettuce on the side.

6 ounces cheddar cheese, shredded (about 1½ cups)
1 fresh green chili, finely chopped
4 slices bread
2 tablespoons butter
Salt and pepper, to taste
Lettuce leaves, for garnish

A tangy, crisp appetizer from northern India, best eaten with finely sliced onion rings. In Bombay, this dish is so popular that it is sold from many street stalls— in the evening it is not uncommon to see people standing around a handcart eating freshly cooked, fried fish. It is served with a mint chutney and a roti.

FISH AMRITSARI

Punjabi fried fish with lemon

1. Mix the ginger-garlic paste, lemon juice, and coarse salt, and marinate the fish in the mixture.

2. In a separate bowl, combine the chickpea flour, ajowan, egg, and chili powder with water to make a thick batter.

3. After 20 minutes, lift the fish out of the marinating mixture and coat each fillet with batter.

4. Heat the oil in a large, heavy frying pan and fry the fillets until crisp.

5. Serve hot with lemon wedges.

1 teaspoon ginger-garlic paste

1 tablespoon lemon juice

Coarse or kosher salt, to taste

4 fillets of fish (cod or similar firm white fish)

2 tablespoons chickpea flour

Pinch ajowan (ajwain)

1 egg

½ teaspoon very red mild chili powder

Sunflower oil for deep-frying

Lemon wedges, for serving

Preparation time: 10 minutes + 20 minutes marinating

Cooking time: 10 minutes

Ratnagiri is not too far from Bombay. It is lush with coconut trees and enjoys a rich seafood cuisine. In India, crabs, caught from the sea as well as from the many rivers, are plentiful and quite cheap. This recipe combines the key ingredients from the area. I love it for its sheer glamour, and often use prepared crabs to save the bother of cleaning fresh ones.

KHEKDA RATNAGIRI
garlic pepper crab

1. Remove all the crabmeat from the shells and pincers, taking care to extract any tiny bits of shell. Mix together the white and the brown meats. Thoroughly rinse the shells and let drain.

2. Heat the oil in a saucepan and add the mustard seeds. When they begin to pop, add the onion and stir until translucent.

3. Add the curry leaves and garlic paste. Stir.

4. Add the coconut and crabmeat and stir lightly until heated through. Season to taste.

5. Pile the mixture into the cleaned crab shells, garnish with some chopped cilantro if you like, and serve warm on a bed of lettuce.

Preparation time: 10 minutes   Cooking time: 10 minutes

4 freshly cooked crabs, shells set aside

2 tablespoons sunflower oil

¼ teaspoon mustard seeds

1 medium onion, finely chopped

5 curry leaves

½ teaspoon garlic paste

1 tablespoon dry coconut

Salt and freshly ground black pepper, to taste

Freshly chopped cilantro (optional)

Lettuce leaves

MURGI NA FARCHA

parsi-style fried chicken

1. Mix together the tomato paste, garam masala, ginger-garlic paste, chili powder, and salt.

2. Place the chicken drumsticks in a saucepan, cover with the tomato-spice mixture and a few tablespoons of water. Cook for about 10 minutes over high heat; reduce the heat when the mixture begins to boil; continue cooking, turning occasionally, until the chicken is three-quarters done.

3. Cool, then roll each drumstick first in bread crumbs, then in beaten eggs, and deep-fry in hot oil in a deep-sided, heavy frying pan or wok until crisp and golden brown. Drain on paper towels.

4. Serve hot, with ketchup, if you like.

4 tablespoons tomato paste
½ teaspoon garam masala
2 teaspoons ginger-garlic paste
½ teaspoon chili powder
Salt, to taste
8 chicken drumsticks, skinned
1¾ ounces (1 cup) fresh bread crumbs
2 eggs, beaten
Sunflower oil for deep-frying
Ketchup (optional)

Preparation time: 10 minutes   Cooking time: 25 minutes

MANPASAND SEEKH

skewered lamb in spices

1. Combine all the ingredients except the lamb in a large bowl and mix well. Add the lamb, stir to coat, and marinate the mixture overnight.

2. The following day, thread the lamb pieces onto skewers and cook under a hot broiler, turning frequently, for 10–15 minutes or until the meat is cooked. Baste occasionally with the marinade.

3. Heat the remaining marinade in a saucepan and serve on the side as a dipping sauce.

⅔ cup plain yogurt
1 small onion, grated
1 teaspoon garam masala powder
1 teaspoon ginger-garlic paste
1 teaspoon chili powder
Salt, to taste
10 ounces lean lamb steak, diced (about 2 cups)

Preparation time: 15 minutes + overnight marinating   Cooking time: 15 minutes

This simple appetizer is a glamorous whirl of color and texture, and tastes especially fresh and clean. It is wonderful for lunch and can easily be made well in advance. It is delicious in the summer with some crusty bread, but it also looks delightful in the winter if you can find some really good out-of-season tomatoes. An added bonus is that it is so simple to make!

TAMATER MAHAL

tomato castles

1. Place eight of the thickest slices of tomato on a serving plate. Top each one with a slice of cheese, then a couple of slices of avocado and red onion, and build up the layers until all the ingredients are used, to make the castle effect.

2. Combine all the ingredients for the dressing and mix well. Drizzle the dressing over the tomato castles and serve with warm, crusty, garlic bread.

Preparation time: 10 minutes

2 large, very red beef tomatoes, thickly sliced

5 ounces mozzarella or similar cheese, such as mild cheddar, sliced

1 ripe, firm avocado, cut into medium-size slices

1 medium red onion, sliced

FOR THE DRESSING

2 tablespoons sunflower oil

2 tablespoons lemon juice

½ teaspoon honey

¼ teaspoon coarsely ground black pepper

¼ teaspoon dry ginger powder

Salt, to taste

1 teaspoon finely chopped cilantro

PALAK ALOO BHAJIA

spinach and potato fritters

1. Combine all the ingredients except the oil in a bowl, and add enough water to make a thick batter.

2. Heat the oil in a large, heavy frying pan and drop in a tablespoonful of mixture. Cook, turning, until lightly browned on both sides. Drain on paper towels and keep warm while you make the rest.

3. Continue to fry the fritters in batches until the batter is used up, and serve hot.

Preparation time: 10 minutes

8 ounces fresh spinach leaves chopped (about 2 cups)
1 cup grated potato
½ teaspoon ground nutmeg
¾ cup chickpea flour
Salt and pepper, to taste
Sunflower oil for deep-frying

METHI MUTHIYAS

baked fenugreek crispies

1. Combine all the ingredients in a mixing bowl and knead into a soft dough, using a little water.

2. Divide the dough into eight equal portions, mold into longish barrel shapes on your palm.

3. Place on a greased baking tray and bake in a preheated oven at 400°F for about 8 minutes, or until crisp and golden in color.

4. Serve hot with a wedge of lemon.

Preparation time: 10 minutes   Cooking time: 8 minutes

1 tablespoon dried fenugreek leaves
5 tablespoons whole-wheat flour
5 tablespoons chickpea flour
¼ teaspoon ginger paste
¼ teaspoon garam masala
1 teaspoon sugar
1 tablespoon sunflower oil
Salt, to taste
Lemon wedges, for serving

Mushrooms are a recent addition to the Indian vegetable market. Now they are so popular that vast farms have been developed for their cultivation. Indian recipes usually call for button or white mushrooms. This one is an easily put together dish for unexpected visitors. Its simplicity and spicy flavor make it a favorite cocktail snack or appetizer.

MASALA MUSHROOMS

mushrooms with chili and garlic

1. Combine the chili powder, garlic paste, cumin powder, oil, and salt in a bowl. Add the mushrooms and lightly stir until well coated.

2. Spread the mushrooms on a heat-proof tray and broil under medium heat for a few minutes until they soften and turn slightly dark. Serve hot with wedges of lemon.

Preparation time: 10 minutes

¼ teaspoon chili powder

½ teaspoon garlic paste

½ teaspoon cumin powder

2 tablespoons olive oil

Onion salt, to taste

10 ounces mushrooms cleaned and cut in half (about 3 cups)

Lemon wedges, for serving

INDIANS USE A VARIETY OF MILK PRODUCTS. YOGURT, OR *DAHI,* IS EATEN ALL OVER INDIA AND, ALONG WITH SOFT RICE, FORMS THE STAPLE DIET OF EVEN VERY LITTLE CHILDREN. IT IS EXCELLENT FOR THE DIGESTION AND MOST INDIANS WILL SAY THAT A MEAL IS INCOMPLETE WITHOUT AT LEAST A SPOONFUL OF YOGURT.

Raitas are salads mixed into yogurt. The yogurt adds a tang and smoothness and provides a cool blandness to counteract the spice in the rest of the meal. *Raitas* are made with raw vegetables like carrot or cucumber, cooked ones such as potatoes or beets, with fruits such as pineapple or orange, or simply with herbs—mint, for example.

In southern India, people eat yogurt at the end of the meal, usually with rice and a hot pickle. In the north, it is drunk throughout the meal in the form of *lassi,* made by mixing yogurt and water. An Indian meal will almost always include a salad or *raita* for color, texture, and fiber. Salads combine vegetables, fruit, and nuts, and are eaten with the main meal. They are simple to make, take no time at all, and complement all Indian food.

SALADS
AND
RAITAS

This is a popular roadside snack in India. On their way home, office workers can be seen outside train stations eating platefuls of watermelon, papaya, chikoo (known as sapota outside India), and bananas. Chaat can also be served with any spicy meat or chicken dish to neutralize the fire.

FRUIT CHAAT
spiced fruit salad

2–2½ cups mixed fresh fruit (choose firm ones such as mango, apple, pear, whole grapes, banana, papaya, or melon), diced

¼ teaspoon chili powder

1 teaspoon lemon juice

1 teaspoon honey

½ teaspoon coarse or kosher salt

Lightly mix all the ingredients together, chill, then serve.

Preparation time: 10 minutes

Dudhi is a long, fat, pale green vegetable belonging to the gourd family. It has spongy but firm white flesh and tastes rather bland, which makes it very versatile. It is sometimes used to thicken vegetable soups. You can remove the skin, as you would for pumpkin. (Pumpkin can be substituted, but dudhi is widely found in Indian food stores.) The mint adds a refreshing zing to this raita, which goes well with meat.

DUDHI PUDINE KA RAITA

dudhi and mint raita

5 ounces dudhi, peeled and grated (about 1 cup)

7 ounces plain yogurt

1 teaspoon bottled mint sauce

¼ teaspoon roasted ground cumin

Salt, to taste

1. Put the dudhi in a heat-proof bowl. Pour in just enough boiling water to cover it. Sweat the dudhi for 2–3 minutes. Drain and let cool.

2. Combine the yogurt, mint sauce, cumin powder, and salt, and beat for one minute.

3. Tip in the drained dudhi, stir, and serve immediately.

Preparation time: 10 minutes

Chickpeas are very popular in northern India, where they are made into a curry and eaten with huge fried bread disks called bhaturas. This chickpea salad adds instant color and texture to a meal and can make a great picnic dish with garlic bread.

CHANA RANGEELA

colorful chickpea salad (right)

One 15-ounce can chickpeas, drained and rinsed

5 tablespoons diced peppers (mixed colors)

1 medium onion, chopped

Coarse or kosher salt, to taste

Generous pinch roasted cumin powder

Generous pinch sugar

2 teaspoons lemon-infused olive oil

2 teaspoons cilantro, finely chopped

Combine the chickpeas with the rest of the ingredients. Serve at room temperature.

Preparation time: 10 minutes

MURG AUR KAJU KA SALAAD

chicken and cashew nut salad

8 ounces cooked chicken

1 small can pineapple chunks, juice reserved

1 cup cashews

5 tablespoons plain yogurt

1 tablespoon cilantro, finely chopped

Salt, to taste

1. Combine the chicken, pineapple, cashews, yogurt, and cilantro. Stir in 3 tablespoons of the pineapple juice. Mix well.

2. Chill, and add salt just before serving.

Preparation time: 10 minutes

This unusual salad introduces a smoky flavor that is not common in Indian vegetarian cooking. It is very popular among the farmers of western India, who eat it with a fat millet bread called bhakri, some garlic chutney, and a slice of raw onion. You can also put little dollops of it on top of savory biscuits, to serve as an appetizer or with drinks.

VANGYACHE BHAREET

roasted eggplant in yogurt

Preparation time: 10 minutes

Cooking time: 15 minutes

1. Brush the eggplant with oil and place under a broiler (be sure you put a pan underneath to collect the juice). Roast, turning from time to time, until soft.

2. Discard the juice. Let the eggplant cool slightly, then peel off the skin. This will have become paper-crisp and should come off easily.

3. Mash the eggplant flesh with a fork, then add the remaining ingredients.

4. Serve cold on a bed of lettuce or on crackers.

1 large eggplant
Sunflower oil for brushing
1 medium onion, chopped finely
1 medium green chili, chopped
1 tablespoon chopped cilantro
⅔ cup plain yogurt
Salt, to taste
¼ teaspoon sugar

The western coastline of India is green with mango farms, where countless varieties of the fruit grow. In summer, pickers load the fruit into vans to transport to the cities, where they are sold for high prices. The firm-fleshed, fragrant Alphonso is the king, but any number of wild mangoes, all sweet and juicy, are used in the cooking of this part of the country.

AAM KA SASAM

wild mango and coconut salad

8 ounces (2¾ cups) dry,
    unsweetened coconut

¼ teaspoon mild chili powder

3 tablespoons dark brown sugar

½ teaspoon whole-grain mustard

Salt, to taste

8 ounces (1 cup) ripe mango,
    peeled, pitted and cubed

1. Combine the coconut, chili powder, sugar, mustard, salt, and a couple of teaspoons of water to dissolve the sugar. Stir until well blended.

2. Add the mango. Stir, and serve chilled.

Preparation time: 15 minutes

Strawberries are available all over India from November until March, when the weather is suitable for their harvest. They are grown in cool hill stations on strawberry farms that make their own brands of jam and juice. This colorful salad brings cheer to summer parties and barbecues. The sweetness of the berries complements spicy chicken dishes beautifully.

KHATTA MEETHA SALAD

berry salad

1 cup strawberries, hulled and halved
1 cup raspberries, hulled
One 12-ounce carton alfalfa sprouts

FOR THE DRESSING
¼ cup orange juice
Coarse or kosher salt, to taste
Pinch freshly crushed black
   peppercorns

Preparation time: 15 minutes

1. Combine the berries and the alfalfa sprouts.

2. Mix the ingredients of the dressing until well blended, and drizzle over the fruit.

3. Serve cold, preferably on a bed of mixed lettuce leaves.

This is such a simple yet popular salad and it goes with any Indian meal. It is made all over India as the ingredients are universally available. It is so fresh and bright to look at, it resembles a bowl of jewels on the dinner table. Any leftovers can be drained of the dressing and used as a sandwich filling.

TAMATER KHEERE KA KACHUMBER
tomato and cucumber jewel salad

1. Combine all the ingredients and serve immediately.

2. If you need to prepare this salad in advance, make the dressing of lemon juice, salt, sugar, and pepper separately, and stir into the vegetables at the last moment.

Preparation time: 10 minutes

1 scant cup ripe, red tomatoes, chopped

1 cup cucumber, peeled and diced

2 tablespoons lemon juice

Salt, to taste

½ teaspoon sugar

¼ teaspoon crushed black peppercorns

ALOO CHAAT

sweet and sour potatoes tossed in spices (right)

1. Combine the dissolved tamarind and sugar, and heat, stirring, until well blended and slightly thick. Cool, and set aside.

2. Arrange the cooked potatoes in a serving dish. Drizzle with the tamarind mixture.

3. Sprinkle with chili powder, coarse salt, and ground cumin.

4. Serve at room temperature, topped with crisp Bombay mix.

Preparation time: 15 minutes   Cooking time: 10 minutes

2 tablespoons tamarind paste or pulp, dissolved in ⅔ cup water

2 tablespoons dark brown sugar

2 cups potatoes, boiled and cubed

¼ teaspoon chili powder

Coarse or kosher salt, to taste

¼ teaspoon roasted ground cumin

3 tablespoons crisp Bombay mix
(a spicy mixture of nuts, lentils, and fired gram four noodles, available at specialty Indian food stores)

PANEER KA RAITA

cottage cheese and crouton salad

1. Arrange a bed of lettuce on a serving dish. Gently pile the paneer cubes on top.

2. To make the dressing, whisk together the yogurt, cheese, garlic, and onion salt until smooth.

3. Pour the dressing over the paneer and lettuce. Serve at once, topped with garlic croutons.

Preparation time: 15 minutes

10 ounces salad mix

10 ounces (2¼ cups) paneer (Indian cottage cheese), cubed

FOR THE DRESSING

⅔ cup plain yogurt

2 tablespoons cream cheese

¼ teaspoon garlic paste

Onion salt, to taste

2 tablespoons garlic croutons

Beets are a favorite salad vegetable in India, and you can see really large ones in the markets. They are served raw or cooked. This salad makes a lovely centerpiece on a dinner table because of its beautiful mauve color. For maximum effect, serve chilled in a bowl with a few purple orchids curved around the rim.

CHUKANDAR KA RAITA

beet raita

5 ounces (¾ cup) cooked beets, cubed

1 green chili, chopped finely

1 scant cup plain yogurt, beaten

Salt, to taste

1 teaspoon sugar

Combine all the ingredients, chill, and serve.

Preparation time: 10 minutes

THE LARGE TRIANGLE OF LAND THAT FORMS THE SOUTHERN PENINSULA OF INDIA IS SURROUNDED BY THREE GREAT SEAS: THE ARABIAN SEA ON THE WEST, LAPPING AT THE BEACHES OF MUMBAI, WHERE I LIVE; THE INDIAN OCEAN TO THE SOUTH, CONNECTING US WITH THAT PARADISE ON EARTH SRI LANKA; AND THE BAY OF BENGAL, A SOURCE OF GREAT DELIGHT TO THE BENGALIS WHO LOVE THEIR FISH SO MUCH.

Every coastal town has its fish market. The fisherfolk cast their nets at night and bring back a mind-boggling variety of fish and seafood at daybreak. The biggest fish market in Mumbai is at Sasoon Dock. Trawlers and boats carrying all kinds of fish—including shark, pomfret, prawns, shrimp, lobsters, and crabs—arrive at 5 A.M. The biggest fish and the best shellfish are taken away by restaurateurs. Then the fisherwomen sort the rest of the catch by hand, put it into baskets, and start to sell it. There is plenty of bargaining, and by 11 A.M. the fish is all sold, the market bare.

In India's interior regions, there are plenty of rivers filled with fat orange and silver fish, such as mandli, hilsa, and rohu, and black crabs. The flesh of river fish is sweeter in taste than that of sea fish. The Bengalis love freshwater fish, but saltwater species are preferred in southern India.

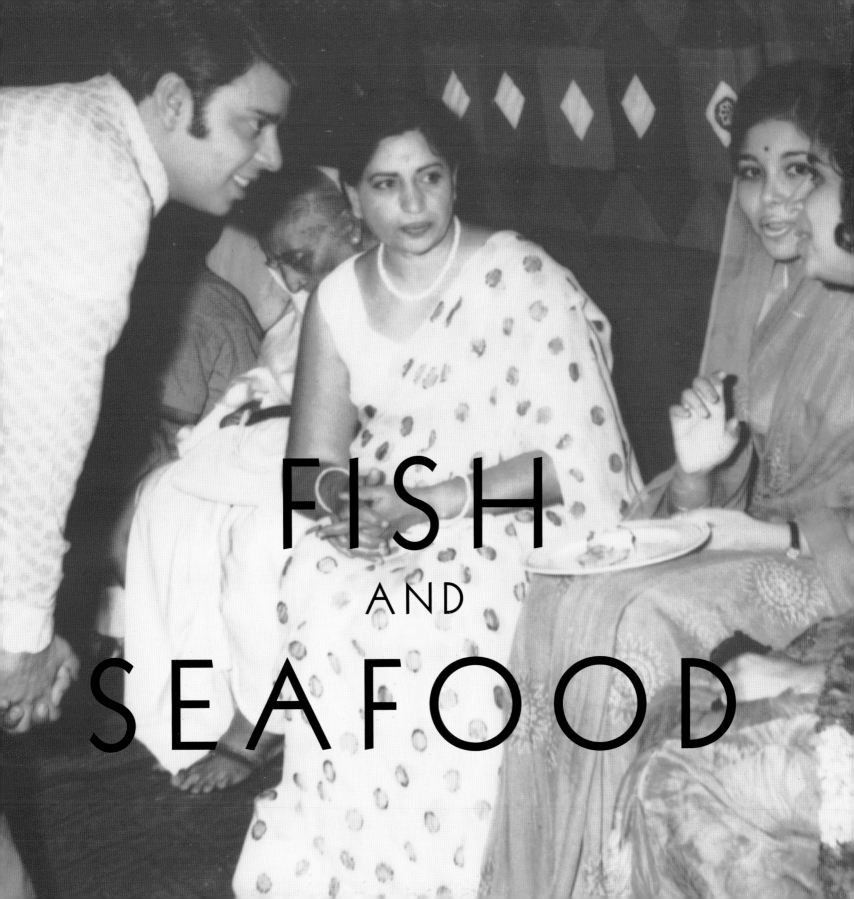

FISH

AND

SEAFOOD

This recipe is from my grandmother's kitchen. These deliciously prepared shrimp can also be bought from little stalls on the beaches of Bombay. I have wonderful memories of eating them out of little paper cones, watching the sun dip into the darkening Arabian Sea.

JHINGA KURKURE

bombay crisp garlic shrimp (right)

1. Mix together all the ingredients of the marinade and gently stir in the shrimps. Set aside.

2. Heat the oil in a large frying pan.

3. Roll the shrimp in the semolina and place a few at a time into the oil when it is smoking hot. Reduce the heat and fry the shrimp for a couple of minutes on each side until done.

4. Remove and drain on paper towels; keep warm while you cook the remaining shrimp.

5. Serve hot, accompanied by a crisp green salad or plain boiled rice and Cumin and Pepper Curry (see page 106).

FOR THE MARINADE
½ teaspoon turmeric
½ teaspoon chili powder
½ teaspoon garlic paste
Salt, to taste

1¼ pounds large uncooked shrimps, shelled
Sunflower oil for frying
6 tablespoons semolina

Preparation time: 5 minutes + 15 minutes marinating
Cooking time: 15 minutes

Although shellfish abound in the coastal waters around India, prawns are a national favorite. Some varieties can be up to eight inches long. This recipe is for an exotic-looking dish full of flavor and zing. Enjoy it on its own or with nan or roti to soak up the delicious cilantro sauce.

JALPARI HARA MASALA

shrimp in green herbs

1. Put the ingredients for the masala in a blender and purée until smooth. Set aside.

2. Heat the oil in a wok and tip in the cumin seeds.

3. Add the green masala and fry for 1–2 minutes.

4. Add the shrimp and salt. Reduce the heat and cook until the shrimp are done, adding a little water if necessary. The sauce should be thick and smooth. Serve immediately.

Preparation time: 10 minutes   Cooking time: 10 minutes

FOR THE GREEN MASALA

1 bunch cilantro

2 fresh green chilies

2 teaspoons ginger-garlic paste

Salt, to taste

2 tablespoons sunflower oil

½ teaspoon cumin seeds

1¼ pounds jumbo shrimp, shelled and deveined

Salt, to taste

This dish is from southern India, which is dotted with coffee and eucalyptus plantations. Creepers of pepper climb the trees and fill the air with a spicy aroma. In this recipe, the piquancy of green peppercorns (I use the bottled ones pickled in brine) and the sharpness of black ones provide an irresistible combination of flavors.

JHINGA MIRIWALE

tiger shrimp and pepper fry

1. Heat the oil and drop in the chilies, black peppercorns, and anise. Stir for one minute.

2. Tip in the shallots and garlic paste, and stir. Add the tomato paste and salt. Blend together.

3. Mix in the tiger shrimp and toss until well sealed on all sides.

4. Add 4 tablespoons water and cook until shrimp are done.

5. Serve hot, sprinkled with green peppercorns.

Preparation time: 10 minutes   Cooking time: 10 minutes

2 tablespoons sunflower oil

8 dried red Kashmiri chilies, broken in half (if unavailable, use other mild red chili)

1 teaspoon black peppercorns, crushed

1 teaspoon anise

12 shallots, chopped

1 teaspoon garlic paste

1 tablespoon tomato paste

Salt, to taste

1¼ pounds tiger shrimp, shelled and cleaned

1 tablespoon pickled green peppercorns

*This recipe captures the laid-back ambience of Goa's sun-drenched beaches.
Kabobs are popular all over India and are sold at many street stalls. The addition
of peppers adds drama. Cut the peppers and onions into chunks roughly the size
of the shrimp. Serve the kabobs with a roti and a salad.*

JHINGA KABOB

crisp shrimp kabobs

1. Combine all the ingredients of the marinade and soak the shrimp in it for 15 minutes. Set aside.

2. Thread the shrimp, peppers, and onion alternately on the skewers until each resembles a colorful ribbon. Brush with oil. Place under a medium-hot broiler and cook for 20 minutes, turning over halfway through cooking. Serve hot.

Preparation time: 10 minutes + 15 minutes marinating
Cooking time: 25 minutes

FOR THE MARINADE
2 tablespoons lemon juice
½ teaspoon turmeric
½ teaspoon chili powder
½ teaspoon garlic paste
Salt, to taste

1¼ pounds large uncooked
  shrimp, shelled
1 cup mixed peppers, cut
  into large chunks
1 cup onions, cut into large
  chunks

8 skewers

MACCHI LAHSUNI

salmon with garlic crumb (right)

1. Brush the seasoned salmon with a little of the oil and grill in a ridged grill pan for about 10 minutes.

2. Meanwhile, heat the remaining oil in a frying pan, add the bread crumbs, garlic paste, nuts, turmeric, and onion salt. Cook until deep golden, stirring continuously.

3. Spoon the crumb mixture over the fish and serve immediately.

Preparation time: 5 minutes   Cooking time: 10 minutes

4 salmon steaks, seasoned with salt
2 tablespoons sunflower oil
2 cups bread crumbs
¼ teaspoon garlic paste
2 tablespoons broken cashews
½ teaspoon turmeric
Onion salt, to taste

CHUTNEY NI MACCHI

flounder with mint chutney

1. Place all the ingredients for the chutney in a food processor and blend to a fine paste, adding a tablespoon of water if necessary.

2. Smear each fillet of fish with a little chutney and wrap individually in banana leaves or foil. Steam for 10 minutes. (There is no need for them to be in a single layer.)

3. Serve, still wrapped, although note that banana leaves are not edible. This goes well with rice and Lentil and Vegetable Purée (see page 102).

Preparation time: 15 minutes   Cooking time: 10 minutes

FOR THE CHUTNEY
1 ounce (2 cups) pineapple mint leaves
½ ounce fresh cilantro
2 green chilies
1 tablespoon ginger-garlic paste
½ teaspoon turmeric
3 tablespoons white distilled malt vinegar
Pinch sugar
Salt, to taste
3¾ x 2½ x 1-inch block of creamed coconut

8 flounder fillets, seasoned with salt
8 banana leaves (optional)

Imagine sitting on a beach with a glass of beer and a bowl of this lobster curry and fluffy rice . . . perfect. The piquant flavor makes this curry great for Sunday lunch, after which a siesta is compulsory! The area of Konkan along the western coast of India is well known for exotic seafood cuisine that combines ingredients such as coconut, raw mango, and kokum, a sour dried fruit. In recent years, many Konkani restaurants have opened up all over India.

KONKANI LOBSTER KADHI

coastal lobster curry

1. Heat one tablespoon oil and fry half the onion slices until brown. Add the coconut, stir, and remove from the heat.

2. Cool the mixture slightly and blend to a paste in a food processor. Set aside.

3. Heat the rest of the oil and drop in the remaining onion slices. Stir until translucent, then add the garlic paste. Quickly stir, then add the tomato paste, garam masala, turmeric, chili powder, and salt. Blend. Add 1¼ cups hot water and bring to a boil.

4. Drop in the lobster, return to a boil, then reduce the heat to a simmer. Heat through for 5 minutes, and serve with boiled rice.

3 tablespoons sunflower oil
2 medium onions, sliced
¼ cup dry, unsweetened coconut
2 tablespoons garlic paste
1 tablespoon tomato paste
1 teaspoon garam masala
½ teaspoon turmeric
½ teaspoon chili powder
Salt, to taste
1¼ pounds cooked lobster in shell, cut into pieces

Preparation time: 10 minutes **Cooking time:** 15 minutes

BHUJANE

sweet and sour fish

1. Marinate the fish in a mixture of the chili, turmeric, garlic paste, salt, and tamarind.

2. Heat the oil in a flat, low-sided pan, and add the onion. Stir until translucent.

3. Add the fish and cook gently, turning over, until done (about 10 minutes for cod). Do not cover as the steam would destroy the perfect texture and consistency of the dish.

Preparation time: 15 minutes + 15 minutes marinating   Cooking time: 10 minutes

8 fillets of fish

1 teaspoon chili powder

1 teaspoon turmeric powder

1 teaspoon garlic paste

Salt, to taste

1 tablespoon tamarind paste or pulp, dissolved in 2 tablespoons water

¼ cup sunflower oil

4 large onions, chopped finely

BHARLELI KALWA

stuffed mussels

1. Blend the ingredients for the masala to a smooth green paste in a coffee grinder or small blender. Set aside.

2. Heat the oil and fry the onion until golden. Add the tomato and salt. Stir.

3. Add the green masala paste and stir until blended.

4. Spoon a little of this mixture over each mussel. Sprinkle with a little cheese and put under a hot broiler until the cheese just begins to melt.

5. Serve immediately on a bed of lettuce, garnished with wedges of lemon.

Preparation time: 15 minutes   Cooking time: 10 minutes

FOR THE GREEN MASALA

3 cups fresh cilantro

2 tablespoons bottled mint sauce

1 teaspoon ginger-garlic paste

4 green chilies

1 teaspoon garam masala

2 tablespoons sunflower oil

2 tablespoons finely chopped onion

2 tablespoons finely chopped tomato

Salt, to taste

16 cooked mussels in shell

3 tablespoons grated cheddar cheese

Lettuce leaves and lemon wedges, for serving

Not surprisingly, the coastal people of India eat a diet that consists mainly of seafood and rice. This recipe comes from the state of Maharashtra on the western coast of India and is made by a community called the Saraswats.

TISRYA SUKKE

clams with dry coconut

1. Heat the oil in a saucepan and fry the onion until golden. Add chilies, ginger-garlic paste, and tomato, and stir until mushy.

2. Tip in the garam masala, turmeric, and coconut, and mix thoroughly.

3. Gently stir in the clams, season with salt, and serve hot with rotis.

Preparation time: 10 minutes   Cooking time: 5 minutes

3 tablespoons sunflower oil

2 onions, chopped finely

2 green chilies, slit lengthwise

1 teaspoon ginger-garlic paste

1 medium tomato, chopped

1 teaspoon garam masala

½ teaspoon turmeric

¾ cup dry, unsweetened coconut

10 ounces cooked clams (the shelled ones sold in cans or jars are suitable, in which case, use a heaped cup)

Salt, to taste

The combination of fish and mustard is a favorite in Bengal. Bengalis truly enjoy their seafood and swear by the fish in their local rivers. They are especially fond of the rohu and hilsa, and fantasize about these delicacies when away from home. I have altered this recipe a bit to make it quick and easy, but it is just as delicious as the original, which is roasted in banana leaves.

MAACH PATURI

bengali fish in mustard sauce

1. Combine the mustard, turmeric, chili powder, salt, and oil.

2. Smear the paste over the fish and place on a greased baking tray. Bake in a preheated oven at 375°F for 10 minutes.

3. Serve hot with rice and a sweet and sour pickle.

Preparation time: 10 minutes   Cooking time: 10 minutes

2 tablespoons whole-grain mustard

1 teaspoon turmeric

½ teaspoon chili powder

Salt, to taste

2 tablespoons sunflower oil

8 fillets of cod or similar firm white fish

This recipe, from the state of Karnataka, is for those with mouths of steel who dare to order the hottest curry in an Indian restaurant without a trace of hesitation. However, it is really not meant to scorch the palate, only to create a burst of heat, fragrance, and flavor. Sunflower oil can be used if you can't get coconut oil.

AMSHE TIKSHE
fire-hot red fish curry

1. Grind the 20 chilies (yes, 20!), tamarind, and garlic to a fine paste in a blender. Add salt and enough water to obtain a pouring consistency.

2. Bring this mixture to a boil and add the fish. Simmer until the fish is cooked, about 10 minutes for cod.

3. Float the oil on top of the curry and serve hot with boiled rice and poppadums.

Preparation time: 10 minutes   Cooking time: 15 minutes

20 dried red Kashmiri chilies (shake out as many seeds as possible); if unavailable, use a red, mild variety of chili

2 tablespoons tamarind pulp or paste

2 cloves garlic

Salt, to taste

8 fillets of cod or other firm white fish

1 tablespoon coconut oil

This is an easy one-pot supper from Bengal that goes well with plain rice. Many fish-eating communities of India healthfully combine seafood and vegetables. This curry is especially good for the winter because of its oil content. You can use sunflower oil if you cannot find mustard oil.

MACCHI TARKARI

fish and vegetable curry

1. Smear the fish with the onion salt and half the turmeric.

2. Heat oil in a large, heavy frying pan and fry the fish until golden. Reserve and keep warm.

3. Add the rest of the turmeric to the oil and quickly tip in the potatoes. Fry for 1–2 minutes.

4. Add the cauliflower and cook for a few minutes, then add in the tomatoes, coriander, and cumin powders, and fry well.

5. Add ¼ cup water, salt to taste, and bring to a boil.

6. Return the fish to the pan, heat through, and serve immediately.

8 fillets of cod or similar firm white fish

Onion salt, to taste

1 teaspoon turmeric

½ cup mustard oil

5 ounces potatoes, cubed

5 ounces cauliflower florets

4 tomatoes, quartered

1 tablespoon ground coriander

1 tablespoon ground cumin

Salt, to taste

Preparation time: 10 minutes   Cooking time: 15 minutes

MEAT-EATING INDIANS LOVE CHICKEN AND PREFER IT TO ANY OTHER BIRD. GOANS EAT FIERY DUCK CURRIES LACED WITH VINEGAR AND COCONUT, AND SOME STATES HAVE RECIPES FOR GUINEA FOWL OR PIGEON. However, these exotic birds are most often associated with the kitchens of the erstwhile Maharajas of India who loved hunting, or *shikar,* and brought back game birds from the forest, such as peacock or quail, to roast in earthen ovens. The birds were marinated in up to thirty spices and cooked slowly on coal embers.

Some of the most popular culinary exports of India are chicken curries, among them Chicken Tikka Masala and Butter Chicken. There is nothing as wholesome as a simple "chicken curry and rice" to satisfy one's passion for Indian food, but the full chicken repertoire of India is vast and wonderful. In the United Kingdom, many restaurants serve up Balti Chicken or Chicken Madras, which I have never eaten in India. Balti Chicken must have been inspired by a classic dish called Kadhai Chicken. *Balti* means "bucket," but every balti that I've eaten has been served in a *kadhai* or Indian wok.

CHICKEN

Unripe tomatoes are green. They are wonderfully tart and largely used in southern Indian cooking. They are often cooked with potatoes, to accompany a meat dish. Green tomatoes impart a unique tang and color to this simple chicken dish.

MURGH HARA TAMATER

chicken with green tomato

1. Combine the marinade ingredients and put the chicken in the marinade. Set aside for 15 minutes.

2. Meanwhile, heat 2 tablespoons oil in a wok. When hot, drop in the cumin seeds. As they darken, add the onion. Stir until translucent.

3. Add the green tomatoes and ginger paste, and cook until soft and well blended. Add the cilantro and season with salt. Remove from the heat and set aside.

4. Heat the remaining oil in a frying pan. When it is nearly smoking, add the chicken pieces and salt to taste. Stir till done, adding a little water if necessary. This should take no more than 15 minutes—the chicken should be fairly dry.

5. Serve a cluster of chicken breast, topped with a dollop of the green tomato chutney. This dish is best enjoyed with a hot nan, a medley of steamed vegetables, and a fruity salad such as Spiced Fruit Salad (see page 26).

Preparation time: 20 minutes + 15 minutes marinating

Cooking time: 30 minutes

FOR THE MARINADE
2 tablespoons lemon juice
2 teaspoons ginger-garlic paste
½ teaspoon green chili paste
Salt, to taste

1¼ pounds chicken breast, skinned and cut into ½-inch-thick slices
6 tablespoons sunflower oil
¼ teaspoon cumin seeds
5 ounces (1 cup) onion, finely chopped
5 ounces (1 cup) fresh green tomatoes, chopped, or 1–2 tablespoons green tomato chutney
1 teaspoon ginger paste
1 teaspoon finely chopped fresh cilantro
Salt, to taste

Mangalore, on the western coast of India, has produced a distinctive coconut-based cuisine that is popular all over India. This is a classic chicken curry with the fire of chili and the sweetness of coconut. Serve it with rice, as it would be traditionally eaten, or combine it with garlic bread for an unusual twist.

MANGALORE GASSI

chicken with coconut and chili

1. Heat half the oil in a wok and add the onion. Stir until brown.

2. Add the coconut, garam masala, and ginger-garlic paste, and stir until the mixture turns dark. Remove from the heat, let cool, then blend coarsely in a food processor. Set aside.

3. Heat the remaining oil in a wok and add the chicken. Stir it around, then add the chili, turmeric, and salt.

4. Tip in the reserved onion and coconut mixture, add a little water, and let the chicken cook through—about 15 minutes.

5. Complete the dish by stirring in the coconut milk. Serve hot but without boiling, as coconut milk may curdle.

¼ cup sunflower oil

5 ounces (1 cup) onion, sliced

5 ounces (1¾ cups) dry, unsweetened coconut

1 teaspoon garam masala

2 teaspoons ginger-garlic paste

1¼ pounds chicken drumsticks, skinned

¼ teaspoon chili powder

¼ teaspoon turmeric

Salt, to taste

1¼ cups coconut milk

Preparation time: 10 minutes Cooking time: 20 minutes

MOONGPHALI KA MURG

broiled chicken with peanut sauce

1. Smear the chicken breasts with a mixture of onion salt, garlic paste, tandoori masala, and lemon juice.

2. Brush with oil, place under a medium-hot broiler, and cook for 20 minutes, turning after 10.

3. Make the peanut sauce by mixing the peanut butter and pineapple juice in a small pan. Heat gently, stirring until it begins to bubble. Remove from the heat and sprinkle with chopped cilantro, if you like.

4. Serve each chicken breast drizzled with peanut sauce, or serve the sauce in a separate bowl.

Preparation time: 10 minutes   Cooking time: 20 minutes

4 boneless, skinless chicken breasts
Onion salt, to taste
1 teaspoon garlic paste
1 tablespoon tandoori masala powder
2 tablespoons lemon juice
Sunflower oil for brushing
Chopped cilantro (optional)

FOR THE SAUCE
4 tablespoons peanut butter
6 tablespoons pineapple juice

KALI MIRCH MURG (right)

chicken curry with black pepper

1. Heat the oil in a wok. Drop in the bay leaf, cloves, and peppercorns. Stir. Add the ginger-garlic paste.

2. After about 30 seconds, add the chicken and mix it into the spices.

3. Add the turmeric, chili powder, and salt and let the chicken cook in its juices until done.

4. Finish by stirring in the yogurt. Heat through, check seasoning, and serve.

Preparation time: 10 minutes   Cooking time: 20 minutes

2 tablespoons sunflower oil
1 bay leaf
4 cloves
1 teaspoon black peppercorns, roughly crushed
2 teaspoons ginger-garlic paste
1¼ pounds boneless chicken, cubed
½ teaspoon turmeric
½ teaspoon chili powder
Salt, to taste
1¼ cups plain yogurt, beaten

Kashmir, the beautiful Himalayan state in northern India, is full of pine nut trees. The nuts are sent to markets all over India and are used in many sweet and savory recipes. The garnish of this dish is quite special and conjures images of dinners hosted by the Maharajas of India. Regal and yet simple, this chicken recipe can be made in advance and reheated just before serving.

MURGH NIYOZA

chicken with pine nuts

1. Heat the oil and drop in the chilies, then add the ginger-garlic paste. Stir.

2. Mix in the onion and fry until translucent. Add the garam masala, turmeric, and salt. Blend.

3. Stir in the shredded chicken and heat through.

4. Serve hot, sprinkled with the pine nuts, raisins, and chopped mint, to accompany rotis.

Preparation time: 15 minutes   **Cooking time:** 10 minutes

3 tablespoons sunflower oil

2 dried red Kashmiri chilies
(or other mild red chilies)

2 teaspoons ginger-garlic paste

1 medium onion, chopped

1 teaspoon garam masala

1 teaspoon turmeric

Salt, to taste

1¼ pounds cooked chicken,
shredded

2 tablespoons dry-roasted pine nuts

2 tablespoons black raisins

Handful of mint leaves, chopped

The size of India being what it is, the cuisine is varied and endless. People outside the country may be surprised to know that recipes associated with Western cooking have close cousins in the East, as is the case with this lovely recipe from northern India. The original recipe was created in the kitchens of the Mughal rulers of Delhi. Flavored with vineyard-fresh grapes, this is the dish to serve as an elegant meal between friends. You could also use black and green grapes for drama and serve this with pulao rice and Spicy Potato Mash with Onion (see page 84).

MURGH ANGOORI

white chicken curry with green grapes

1. Heat the oil, add the onion, and fry until translucent.

2. Add the ginger-garlic paste and chilies, and stir. Tip in the garam masala, salt, and then the chicken.

3. Fry until the chicken is well sealed on all sides.

4. Pour in the yogurt and coconut milk, and heat gently until the chicken is cooked, adding a little water for a smooth consistency, if necessary.

5. Add the grapes at the last moment to preserve their crisp sweetness, and serve hot.

Preparation time: 15 minutes   Cooking time: 15 minutes

2 tablespoons sunflower oil

1 medium onion, sliced

1 tablespoon ginger-garlic paste

2 green chilies, slit lengthwise

1 teaspoon garam masala

Salt, to taste

1¼ pounds boneless chicken, cubed

⅔ cup plain yogurt, beaten

⅔ cup coconut milk

15 green seedless grapes, halved

This indulgent dish from Delhi goes well with a rice pulao or roti. In days gone by, it would be cooked in ghee, or clarified butter, but more and more people are simplifying their cooking and choosing healthier ingredients. Here, the subtle flavor of chicken is beautifully complemented by the cheese and cream, with a hint of chilies to provide heat.

MURGH MALAI

creamy chicken

1. Heat the oil and fry the ginger-garlic paste for a minute.

2. Add the green chilies, chicken, and salt. Stir until the chicken is half done, adding a little water as necessary.

3. Add the cashew purée and nutmeg, and blend. As it begins to bubble, add the yogurt and cream. Heat through, adding some water for consistency.

4. Serve hot, sprinkled with the cheddar cheese.

Preparation time: 15 minutes   Cooking time: 15 minutes

3 tablespoons sunflower oil

1 tablespoon ginger-garlic paste

2 fresh green chilies, chopped finely

1¼ pounds boneless chicken, cubed

Salt, to taste

¼ cup cashews, ground to a paste with some water

¼ teaspoon ground nutmeg or grated nutmeg

⅔ cup thick, whole-milk yogurt

½ cup heavy cream

3 tablespoons cheddar cheese, shredded

Cardamom is a warming spice, and this recipe is wonderful in the winter. Ground cardamom is readily available, but buy small amounts at a time as it loses flavor quite quickly. Better to buy whole pods, which are longer lasting, and grind the seeds as needed. Cardamom is used in many sweets as well, and is therefore a versatile spice for your pantry. Indian Spiced Tea (page 145) often contains a little ground cardamom.

ELAICHI MURGH

cardamom-flavored chicken

3 tablespoons sunflower oil

1 teaspoon ground cardamom

1¼ pounds boneless chicken, cubed

Salt, to taste

1 teaspoon chili powder

1 teaspoon turmeric

2 teaspoons tomato paste

⅔ cup plain yogurt

1. Heat the oil and lightly fry all but a pinch of the ground cardamom.

2. Add the chicken and salt, and stir until the meat is sealed on all sides.

3. Tip in the spices and tomato paste and mix well.

4. Pour in the yogurt and ⅔ cup water. Bring to a boil, reduce to a low heat, and cook until the chicken is tender.

5. Serve hot, sprinkled with the reserved cardamom, with rice or rotis.

Preparation time: 10 minutes   Cooking time: 20 minutes

India is the world's largest producer of chilies, so it is not surprising that we put them into every savory dish! This one is a variation of a northern recipe. You can vary the amount of chilies according to taste. Nuts are often combined with chicken to add texture and flavor. Serve it with Beet Raita (see page 37) for stunning color contrast.

TIKHI MURGH BADA-MI

chicken with chili almond sauce

1. Place the chicken in the stock and bring to a boil. Simmer until cooked through. Set aside and keep warm.

2. Meanwhile, purée the chilies, garlic paste, bread, almonds, and cilantro in a blender, along with some water.

3. Transfer this mixture to a heavy pan, add salt, and simmer until well blended and thick.

4. To serve, arrange the chicken on a bed of rice, pour the sauce over the top, and drizzle with lemon juice.

Preparation time: 15 minutes   Cooking time: 15 minutes

8 chicken legs, skinned

2 cups chicken stock

4 fresh green chilies

½ teaspoon garlic paste

2 slices white bread, crusts removed

⅔ cup almonds

3 tablespoons chopped cilantro

Salt, to taste

2 tablespoons lemon juice

Boiled rice, for serving

KOZHI CHETTINAD DOSA

spicy fried chicken-stuffed crêpes

1. First make the filling. Heat the oil and add the cumin and anise. As they darken, add the curry leaves.

2. Drop in the onion and let soften. Stir in the ginger-garlic paste.

3. Add the spices, shredded chicken, and salt, and mix well. Heat through and set aside.

4. Make a batter with the flour, salt, and as much water as needed for a pouring consistency.

5. Brush a nonstick frying pan with oil and spoon a ladleful of batter into the center. Spread this into a thin disk using the back of the spoon.

6. Cover, and cook over low heat. Arrange some of the chicken mixture along the center of the crêpes, roll up, and keep it warm while you cook the remaining batter—it should be enough for 12 crêpes.

Preparation time: 15 minutes   Cooking time: 15 minutes

3 tablespoons sunflower oil

1 teaspoon cumin seeds

1 teaspoon anise

8 curry leaves

2 medium onions, chopped

1 tablespoon ginger-garlic paste

½ teaspoon chili powder

1 teaspoon garam masala

10 ounces cooked chicken, shredded

Salt, to taste

CRÊPE BATTER

2½ cups rice flour

Salt, to taste

Water, as necessary

Sunflower oil for brushing

This is the classic chicken curry made in homes all over India. The combination of chicken and tomatoes is pure magic. Often, a boiled, quartered potato is added for extra flavor. You can also dress up this recipe by adding a little cream, nuts, or dried fruits such as apricots or peaches.

LAL TAMATAR MURGH

chicken and red tomato curry

3 tablespoons sunflower oil

1 medium onion, chopped

1 tablespoon ginger-garlic paste

1¼ pounds skinless chicken breasts, kept whole

½ teaspoon turmeric

1 teaspoon garam masala

Salt, to taste

One 14½-ounce can chopped tomatoes

2 tablespoons chopped cilantro

1. Heat the oil in a saucepan and fry the onion until soft.

2. Add the ginger-garlic paste, stir, and add the chicken, stirring to seal on all sides.

3. Once the chicken is sealed, stir in the turmeric, garam masala, and salt. Mix well.

4. Pour in the tomatoes and bring to a boil. Reduce the heat and simmer until the chicken is done, adding a little water if necessary.

5. Serve hot, sprinkled with cilantro. This dish is wonderful served with rice noodles, tossed with chopped cilantro.

Preparation time: 15 minutes   Cooking time: 20 minutes

This special dish is inspired by the cuisine of the Nawabs of Lucknow in northern India. They would flavor their meats with various fruits and flower essences such as rose, vetiver, screw pine, and jasmine. Sandalwood was also used to perfume some dishes. This simple recipe conjures up visions of royal banquets, glittering with jewels and brocade. Enjoy it with rotis.

SAFAID MURGH GULABI

chicken in rose-flavored sauce

1. Heat the oil in a large, heavy frying pan and lightly fry the chicken legs, turning to seal on all sides.

2. Add the yogurt, ginger, chilies, salt, and cardamom. Cover and cook until the chicken is tender.

3. Stir in the ground almonds. Simmer for a couple of minutes, adding a little water if necessary, and remove from the heat.

4. Add the cream and rose essence just before serving.

3 tablespoons sunflower oil
1¼ pounds chicken legs, skinned
⅔ cup plain yogurt, beaten
1 tablespoon ground ginger
2 fresh green chilies, minced
Salt, to taste
½ teaspoon ground cardamom
3 tablespoons ground almonds
⅔ cup heavy cream
½ teaspoon rose essence

Preparation time: 15 minutes   Cooking time: 20 minutes

NEARLY 85 PERCENT OF INDIANS ARE HINDUS, MANY OF WHOM ARE VEGETARIAN BECAUSE THEIR RELIGION RESPECTS ALL FORMS OF LIFE. No Hindu eats meat on festive days or at weddings, whereas Muslims, Zoroastrians, and Christians have meat-rich feasts on such days. Meat-eaters prefer lamb, called mutton in India; only an extremely small number eat beef or pork.

There are endless ways of cooking lamb—as kabobs, in curries, or in various patties. In traditional curries, twenty-five different spices may be used, simmered for hours to draw out flavor, fragrance, and fire from each one. Today, our premixed ground spices, better methods of processing meat so that it cooks faster, and healthier oils mean that modern cooks can whip up nutritious, authentic delicacies in a much shorter time. I usually make my meat curries a day in advance as they taste so much better the next day. Also I make my curries in a pressure cooker, which cuts down cooking times drastically. I know that many people in the West consider this device old-fashioned, but in India, every household has at least a couple of pressure cookers that are used at least several times a day!

LAMB

MUTTONCHA PANDHRA RASSA

lamb in cashew sauce

1. Cut the lamb into strips. Mix together the marinade ingredients and soak the lamb in it for 15 minutes.

2. Heat the oil in a wok. When hot, add the grated onion and stir until it softens. Add the spices. Lift the lamb strips out of the marinade and add to the pan. Stir well until the meat is seared.

3. Add the marinade and the meat stock. Bring to a boil, then reduce the heat and cook until the lamb is done.

4. Stir in the nut paste and the coconut milk. Heat through.

5. Serve hot on a bed of rice noodles and garnish with red chilies, if you like. (You can make the chilies into flowers by slicing each one about six times from the tip almost to the stalk end. Immerse the chilies in ice-cold water for about 20 minutes, and they will unfurl into "flowers.")

Preparation time: 25 minutes + 15 minutes marinating

Cooking time: 30 minutes

1¼ pounds lean, boneless lamb

FOR THE MARINADE

⅔ cup plain yogurt

3 teaspoons ginger-garlic paste

1 teaspoon finely chopped green chilies

Salt, to taste

3 tablespoons sunflower oil

2 large onions, grated and squeezed dry

½ teaspoon ground coriander

½ teaspoon ground cumin

½ teaspoon garam masala

½ cup meat stock

9 ounces cashews, ground to a paste (to make about 2¼ cups)

½ cup coconut milk

This is a classic recipe from the Himalayan state of Kashmir. Historically, Kashmir has been the point of entry into India for many invaders from Central Asia, and Kashmiri cooking reflects the influence of those cuisines. Traditionally, mustard oil or ghee (clarified butter) is used as the cooking medium, but I have chosen the milder-flavored sunflower oil in order to bring out the aroma of the spices.

CHOKHTA

kashmiri roasted lamb

1. Put the lamb, sunflower oil, salt, and asafetida in a heavy pan and heat until sizzling.

2. Cover, and cook over high heat, stirring from time to time.

3. When the oil begins to separate, reduce the heat, add the chili powder and continue to cook until rich brown in color.

4. Add the ginger and a little water, and cook until the meat becomes tender. Serve hot with rotis.

1¼ pounds lean boneless lamb, cubed

¼ cup sunflower oil

Salt, to taste

½ teaspoon asafetida powder (available from specialty Indian grocery stores)

1 teaspoon red chili powder

1 teaspoon ground ginger

Preparation time: 5 minutes   Cooking time: 40 minutes

RISHTA

meatballs with fennel (right)

1. Put the ground lamb, ground ginger, half the ground fennel, and salt in a blender and whiz around once to get a smooth mixture. Form this into golf-ball-size balls, and set aside.

2. Mix the turmeric, garam masala, chili powder, and the remaining ground fennel with 1¼ cups water in a saucepan and bring to a boil. Pour in the oil and season with salt.

3. Gently place the meatballs in the sauce and cook until they are browned and cooked, adding more water as necessary. Baste them from time to time for flavor. The meatballs should be coated with the sauce, not floating in a gravy. Serve hot with rice or noodles.

Preparation time: 15 minutes   Cooking time: 15 minutes

1 pound lean ground lamb
½ teaspoon ground ginger
1 teaspoon ground fennel
Salt, to taste
1 tablespoon turmeric
1 teaspoon garam masala
1 teaspoon chili powder
3 tablespoons sunflower oil

LIVER KI KHATTI KADHI

tangy liver curry

1. Heat the oil and tip in the asafetida. Add the liver at once. Season with salt and stir.

2. Mix the chili powder in a couple of tablespoons of water, and pour into the pan. Add the anise, ginger, and garam masala, and stir. Pour in ⅔ cup water and bring to a boil.

3. Add the tamarind and cook until the liver is done. Serve hot with rotis.

Preparation time: 10 minutes   Cooking time: 20 minutes

3 tablespoons sunflower oil
¼ teaspoon asafetida
1¼ pounds lamb liver, cubed
Salt, to taste
1 teaspoon chili powder
1 teaspoon ground anise seeds
½ teaspoon ground ginger
½ teaspoon garam masala
2 tablespoons tamarind pulp, mixed with a little water to soften

The legacy of the Raj includes a special and distinctive cuisine that is a unique mix of East and West. Pies, puffs, and bakes are still made all over the country, flavored with Indian spices and herbs, and sold at bakeries and small take-out stores. This recipe is so simple to make and yet tastes like a dream. I have often made it for parties, for a large number of people. Omit the lamb for a vegetarian option.

ANGREZI KEEMA BAKE

baked ground lamb with potatoes

1. Boil the sliced potatoes in salted water until just done. Drain and set aside.

2. Heat the oil and fry the onion until soft. Stir in the garlic and ground allspice.

3. Add the ground lamb and salt. Stir and break up the meat, and cook for 10 minutes.

4. Layer half the potatoes in a buttered ovenproof dish, and season with salt. Cover with the lamb, then a layer of cheese. Top with the rest of the potatoes and more cheese.

5. Pour cream all over the potatoes, letting it trickle to the bottom of the dish.

6. Bake in a preheated 425°F oven for 10 minutes. Serve at once with Berry Salad (see page 32) and crusty bread.

1 pound 10 ounces potatoes (6–7 medium), peeled and thickly sliced

1 tablespoon sunflower oil

1 medium onion, chopped

1 clove garlic, crushed

1 teaspoon ground allspice

9 ounces lean ground lamb

Salt, to taste

9 ounces (2 cups) cheese, grated (I have used Reblochon, Parmesan, or even cheddar)

⅔ cup light cream

Preparation time: 10 minutes   Cooking time: 25 minutes

I make this very simple curry for my family when I am feeling lazy but still want to give everyone a wholesome treat!

ITWAR MUTTON CURRY

Sunday mutton curry

1. Heat the oil in a wok. When hot, add the onion and stir until it softens. Add the ginger-garlic paste, and give the mixture a good stir. Drop in the lamb and stir well over high heat until the meat is seared.

2. Add the tomato paste. Mix the garam masala in a little water and pour into the lamb mixture. Swirl it around, add a glass of water, and let it cook over slow heat until the lamb is tender, adding more water if necessary.

3. Beat the yogurt until smooth. Add to the curry and bring to a boil. When thoroughly heated, serve on a bed of rice noodles (popular in southern India) or with nans.

3 tablespoons sunflower oil

2 large onions, chopped

4 teaspoons ginger-garlic paste

1¼ pounds lean, boneless
lamb, cut into strips

2 tablespoons tomato paste

2 heaped teaspoons garam masala

⅔ cup plain yogurt

Salt, to taste

Preparation time: 10 minutes   Cooking time: 30 minutes

The Sindhi community came to India from Pakistan many decades ago, and brought with it a cuisine that is now popular all over India. It is full of unlikely combinations that work well together. The caramel in this recipe provides color and flavor rather than sweetness. Serve this rich curry with Colorful Vegetable Pulao (see page 121) or even with croissants! (In India, pav, or soft bread, is often eaten with curries; croissants would be equally delicious.)

ALOO MUTTON SHAKKARWALA

caramelized lamb and potato curry

1. Mix all the ingredients for the marinade and add the lamb. Cover and set aside for 10 minutes.

2. Heat a heavy pan, add the sugar, and let it caramelize.

3. Add the oil and, when hot, add the drained lamb cubes, reserving the marinade.

4. Brown the meat and add the onion. Stir until brown. Add the ginger-garlic paste and tomato paste. Add the potatoes and the marinade. Pour in ⅔ cup boiling water, and cook until the meat and potatoes are tender. Add more water if the curry gets too dry while cooking.

Preparation time: 15 minutes + 10 minutes marinating

Cooking time: 40 minutes

FOR THE MARINADE

⅔ cup plain yogurt

½ teaspoon turmeric

½ teaspoon chili powder

1 teaspoon garam masala

Salt, to taste

10 ounces lean boneless lamb, cubed

2 teaspoons sugar

¼ cup sunflower oil

1 medium onion, chopped

1 tablespoon ginger-garlic paste

2 tablespoons tomato paste

4 potatoes, peeled and quartered

This recipe was introduced to India by the Zoroastrians and has now become part of Indian fare. It is served with a curry and rice or on its own with a salad, or raita. I love to serve these with predinner drinks. If you want to serve as an appetizer, reduce the size of each "cutlet."

LACY CUTLETS

lamb patties coated with lace of egg

1. Put the onion, ginger-garlic paste, bread, chilies, garam masala, salt, cilantro, and ground lamb in a blender and whiz around two or three times until you get a well-blended mixture.

2. Shape the mixture into lemon-size balls and flatten each one slightly.

3. Heat the oil in a deep frying pan. Dip each "cutlet" in the beaten egg and fry until cooked through.

4. Serve with wedges of lemon and Pear Chutney.

Preparation time: 15 minutes   Cooking time: 15 minutes

1 medium onion, chopped

1 teaspoon ginger-garlic paste

2 slices wheat bread

2 green chilies

1 teaspoon garam masala

Salt, to taste

2 tablespoons chopped cilantro

10 ounces lean ground lamb

Sunflower oil for deep-frying

3 medium eggs, beaten and seasoned

Lemon wedges and Pear Chutney (see page 153), for serving

Although this recipe from Andhra Pradesh is usually made into a curry, I have used steaks and roasted peppers for a new, almost Mediterranean twist. The mint and the peppers complement the flavor of the lamb, and I often serve it with couscous tossed with a little mint.

MUTTON SIMLA MIRCH

lamb steaks with roasted peppers

1. Heat the garlic butter and oil together, and fry the steaks, 4 minutes on each side. Add the chili powder, turmeric, mint, and salt, and stir.

2. Pour in 1¼ cups water and bring to a boil. Reduce the heat and cook until the lamb is tender and the water has evaporated. Stir in the roasted peppers and heat through.

3. Serve hot, with lemon wedges.

Preparation time: 10 minutes   Cooking time: 40 minutes

¼ cup garlic butter

2 tablespoons sunflower oil

4 lamb steaks cut from the leg

½ teaspoon chili powder

½ teaspoon turmeric

1 tablespoon mint leaves, chopped

Salt, to taste

One 10-ounce jar roasted pepper strips, drained

In India, pure gold and silver leaf, both known as varq, *are used to decorate sweets and rich rice dishes such as biryanis. They are not expensive because they are made with such a tiny amount of metal. You can find the leaf in Indian food stores as sheets pressed between butter paper. In this recipe, inspired by the* shikar, *or hunting, cuisine of the Maharajas, gold leaf is placed on top to add glamour and sparkle.*

MUTTON SONAWALA

lamb with gold leaf

1. Heat the ghee or butter in a heavy pan. If using butter, let the moisture escape without burning the butter.

2. Add the meat, chili, turmeric, ginger-garlic paste, yogurt, and salt, and bring to a boil. Reduce the heat and cook until meat is tender. Add a little water if the curry dries up. You want a fairly thick sauce.

3. Pour in the rose water and stir.

4. Serve hot, with the gold or silver leaf on top. This goes well with Yogurt Bread (see page 129) and Beet Raita (see page 37).

Preparation time: 10 minutes   Cooking time: 45 minutes

¼ cup ghee or unsalted butter

1¼ pounds lean lamb, cubed

1 teaspoon chili powder

1 teaspoon turmeric

2 teaspoons ginger-garlic paste

1¼ cups thick, whole-milk yogurt

Salt, to taste

2 tablespoons rose water

1 sheet gold leaf (or silver, if gold is difficult to find)

WALK INTO ANY VEGETABLE MARKET IN INDIA AND YOU COULD EASILY SPEND A COUPLE OF HOURS TAKING IN THE COLORS, SCENTS, AND SIGHTS. Over the past few years, an amazing variety of vegetables, now all grown in India, have joined the indigenous ones. Potatoes, tomatoes, okra, spinach, coriander, mint, lemon grass, eggplant, banana flowers, beans, jackfruit, gourds, and plantains—all these sit next to mushrooms, baby corn, mixed peppers, lettuce, and broccoli, which in India are considered exotic and exclusive.

Indian supermarkets cater to busy workers, selling prepared carrots, cauliflower florets, or frozen garden peas, and modern Indians happily stock up on ready-to-cook ingredients. Food manufacturers are just as quick to respond to the need to spend less time on our meals, so that we can use bottled ginger-garlic paste, fruit purées, ground nuts, and have wonderfully fresh paneer (Indian cottage cheese) and yogurt without the overnight hanging of curd or the setting of it with cultures. Thankfully, none of this has led to any real decline in authenticity. Gourmets remain just as discerning and expect the same results, which can now be achieved without the time-consuming effort.

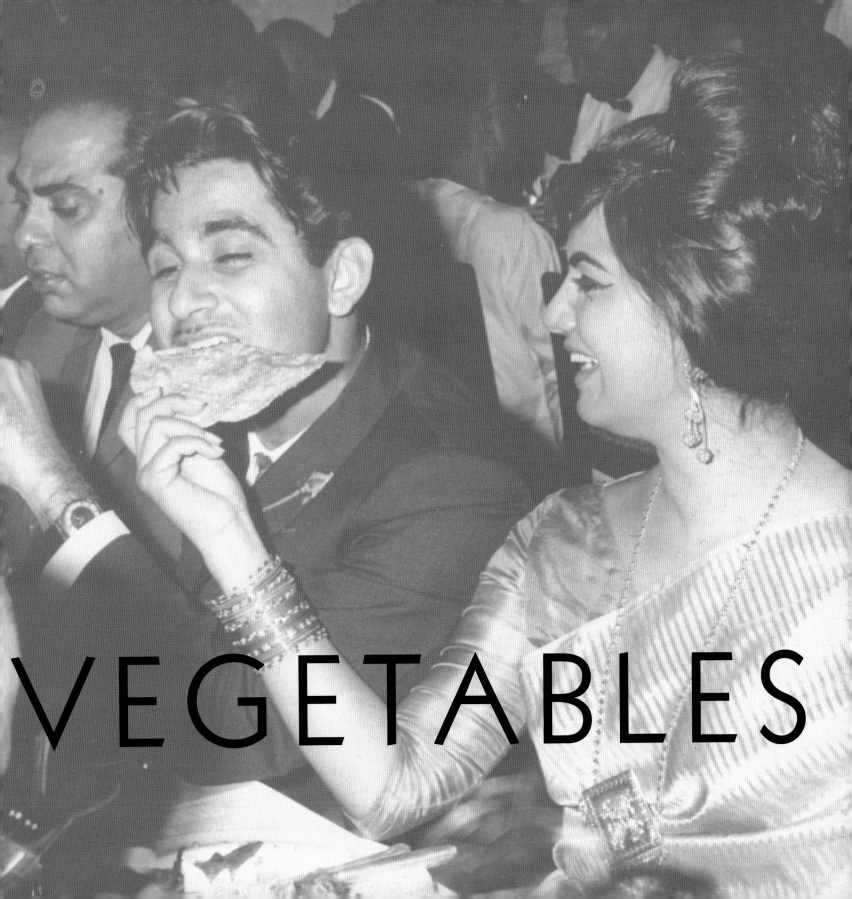

VEGETABLES

Bengalis use this combination of five aromatic spices along with mustard oil in many of their recipes. Here the mild, sweet flavor of squash gets a lift. Black onion seeds are sold as kalonji in Indian shops. You can use any vegetable with this spice mixture for a quick stir-fry. You can use sunflower oil instead of the mustard oil if you prefer, but do select the orange-skinned variety of squash, not the white one.

PANCH PHODONER KADDU

squash with five spices

1. Heat the oil in a large frying pan and add all the spice seeds.

2. As the seeds pop and darken, add the squash, salt, and sugar. Stir and cook over high heat until the squash softens.

3. Serve hot with Banana-Flavored Fried Bread (see page 129). You could chop some red chili over the squash if you want a bit of fire.

Preparation time: 10 minutes   Cooking time: 15 minutes

2 tablespoons mustard oil

½ teaspoon cumin seeds

½ teaspoon fennel seeds

½ teaspoon fenugreek seeds

½ teaspoon black mustard seeds

½ teaspoon black onion seeds

1¼ pounds squash, cubed
  with the skin

Salt, to taste

1 teaspoon sugar

Many Indians will say that a potato subji, or stir-fry, with rotis is the best possible meal they could ever have. There is an amazing variety of potato recipes in every region and always at least one potato dish at festive events. This one is delicious with rotis or as an accompaniment to meat. Any leftovers can be made into pan-fried cakes or mixed with ground meat for kebabs.

BATATA BHAJI

1. Heat a tablespoon of oil and add the mustard seeds.

2. When the seeds pop, add the curry leaves and chili. Stir.

3. Add the mashed potatoes and salt. Blend well and let it heat through. Remove from the heat and keep hot.

4. Heat the remaining oil and fry the onion until golden.

5. Serve the mash, topped with a pile of fried onions and a sprig of cilantro to garnish, if you like.

3 tablespoons sunflower oil

½ teaspoon mustard seeds

A few curry leaves

1 green chili, chopped

4 potatoes, boiled, peeled, and mashed

Salt, to taste

1 large onion, sliced

Sprigs of cilantro, for garnish (optional)

Preparation time: 10 minutes   Cooking time: 20 minutes

The people of Punjab make the most divine paneer (Indian cottage cheese) by hanging clotted milk in cheesecloth until all the liquid has drained away. This recipe makes the most of the smoothness of paneer and the tang of star fruit. Star fruit is grown in many villages in India, but its blandness prevents it from being taken too seriously as a dessert fruit. You will find paneer at all Indian grocers, but you can use ricotta instead if you wish.

PANEER TUKDE

cottage cheese and starfruit with raisin chutney

1. Sprinkle the paneer with the tandoori masala, salt, and lemon juice, and mix lightly. Arrange on a greased tray and place under a medium-hot broiler. Turn over when the paneer begins to change color.

2. Meanwhile, combine all the ingredients for the chutney in a saucepan and bring to a boil, adding a little water if necessary. When the sugar has become syrupy, remove from the heat.

3. To serve, arrange star fruit slices on a plate. Top with the paneer and a dollop of chutney. This makes a good accompaniment to Kashmiri Roasted Lamb (see page 71) and rice.

Preparation time: 10 minutes   Cooking time: 20 minutes

10 ounces paneer or ricotta
½ teaspoon tandoori masala
Salt, to taste
1 tablespoon lemon juice

FOR THE CHUTNEY
3 tablespoons raisins
1 teaspoon brown sugar
2 tablespoons vinegar
Pinch salt

2 large star fruit, sliced

This is a very popular and simple recipe from Bengal. Eggplants are often fried to bring out their flavor, although they absorb a great deal of oil, so drain them well to remove the excess. These crisp eggplant disks with meltingly soft centers are delicious with Lentils with Peanuts (see page 100) and rice.

BHAJA BEGUN

spicy eggplant disks

1 teaspoon turmeric

1 teaspoon red chili powder

1 teaspoon ground cumin

Salt, to taste

¼ cup semolina

2 medium eggplants, sliced

Sunflower oil for frying

Lemon wedges, for serving

Preparation time: 10 minutes

Cooking time: 15 minutes

1. Mix the spices, salt, and semolina.

2. Dip each eggplant slice in this mixture one at a time.

3. Heat the oil in a heavy pan and fry the slices, turning over until both sides are crisp and golden.

4. Remove with a slotted spoon, drain on paper towels, and serve at once with a wedge of lemon.

Makara Sankranti is a Hindu harvest festival in the month of January. Great celebrations are held in the fields, and freshly roasted peanuts mixed with sweet jaggery (molasses made from sugarcane juice) and fruits of the season are eaten. Bullock-cart races entertain the guests. This is a dish from my community of Saraswat Brahmins. It is cooked as part of a Makara Sankranti feast with newly harvested peanuts. Enjoy it as an accompaniment to meat or rice.

KAIRAS

sweet and sour green pepper

1. Heat half the oil in a frying pan and add the sesame seeds. As they darken, drop in the coconut. Stir constantly until the coconut turns golden. Remove from the heat, let cool, and blend the mixture in a coffee grinder or small blender.

2. Heat the remaining oil and add the mustard seeds.

3. When the seeds pop, add the peppers, peanuts, salt, sugar, the softened tamarind, and a little extra water. Cook until the peppers just begin to soften.

4. Stir in the sesame and coconut mixture, and boil once. Remove and serve hot.

Preparation time: 10 minutes   Cooking time: 15 minutes

2 tablespoons sunflower oil

2 tablespoons sesame seeds

2 tablespoons dry, unsweetened coconut

½ teaspoon mustard seeds

3 large green peppers, diced

1 tablespoon whole peanuts

Salt, to taste

2 teaspoons dark brown sugar

1 teaspoon tamarind paste mixed with 1 teaspoon of water to soften

VATANA USAL

green peas stir-fry (right)

1. Heat the oil in a wok and add the cumin seeds.

2. As the seeds darken, tip in the peas and stir.

3. Pour in a little water, add the sugar and salt, and cook without a lid until the peas are tender.

4. Remove from the heat, stir in the coconut, and serve.

Cooking time: 10 minutes

2 tablespoons sunflower oil

½ teaspoon cumin seeds

One 10-ounce package frozen peas

Pinch sugar

Salt, to taste

3 tablespoons dry, unsweetened coconut

FARASBEE UPKARI

green beans with coconut

1. Heat the oil and add the mustard seeds. As they pop, add the cumin and chilies. Stir.

2. Add the green beans, salt, and sugar, and cook until tender.

3. Serve hot, mixed with coconut.

Preparation time: 5 minutes   Cooking time: 15 minutes

2 tablespoons sunflower oil

1 teaspoon mustard seeds

½ teaspoon cumin seeds

2 whole dried red chilies, seeded

1¼ pounds frozen green beans

Salt, to taste

¼ teaspoon sugar

3 tablespoons dry, unsweetened coconut

Farmers in western India eat their lunch in the field and then take a nap under leafy mango and tamarind trees. Their meal often consists of millet rotis, this vegetable stir-fry, a hot pickle, and a knob of jaggery (molasses made from sugarcane juice) or unprocessed sugar. Cabbages have gained an unsavory reputation mainly because they are not cooked correctly, but this fragrant dish really brings out the best in them.

KOBI SIMLACHA ZUNKA

cabbage and green pepper stir-fry

1. Heat a heavy pan and dry-roast the chickpea flour, stirring constantly, for 1 minute. Remove.

2. Heat the oil and add the mustard seeds. As they pop, add the curry leaves. Stir.

3. Drop in the cabbage, green pepper, and salt. Stir until the vegetables begin to wilt.

4. Stir in the roasted flour, crushing any lumps into the vegetables. Cook until well blended and the flour becomes mushy.

5. Serve hot, piled with coconut and a few slit green chilies, if you like.

2 tablespoons chickpea flour

2 tablespoons sunflower oil

1 teaspoon mustard seeds

A few curry leaves

10 ounces (4½–5 cups) cabbage, shredded

10 ounces (1½ cups) green pepper, cut into strips

Salt, to taste

2 tablespoons dry, unsweetened coconut

Green chilies (optional)

Preparation time: 15 minutes   Cooking time: 10 minutes

CAULIFLOWER KA KURMA

baby cauliflower korma

3 tablespoons sunflower oil

1 teaspoon cumin seeds

1 medium onion, chopped

1 teaspoon ginger-garlic paste

1 tablespoon tomato paste

1 teaspoon garam masala

½ teaspoon turmeric

Salt, to taste

½ teaspoon sugar

1¼ pounds baby cauliflower

¼ cup cilantro, chopped

1. Heat the oil in a saucepan. Add the cumin seeds, and as soon as they darken, add the onion. Cook until onion is softened.

2. Add the ginger-garlic paste and tomato paste and stir. Tip in the spices. Cook until well blended.

3. Add the salt and sugar. Place the whole cauliflower in the sauce and baste it. Add ⅔ cup boiling water and cover the pan.

4. Allow the cauliflower to just soften—don't let it become mushy. Serve hot with cilantro sprinkled on top.

Preparation time: 15 minutes Cooking time: 15 minutes

This recipe comes from Uttar Pradesh, home of the magnificent Taj Mahal. The cuisine of this state is delicate and the sweets are legendary. Here, okra is fried to a crunch. Mango powder is made by finely grinding sun-dried unripe mangoes, but you can find it in powdered form sold as amchoor in Indian food shops. Use any leftovers from this dish crumbled over other vegetarian recipes for extra flavor and texture.

BHINDI KURKURE

crisp okra tossed in spices

1 teaspoon red chili powder

1 teaspoon turmeric

½ teaspoon mango powder (amchoor)

Salt, to taste

3 tablespoons chickpea flour

1¼ pounds okra, sliced diagonally (about 2½ cups)

Sunflower oil for deep-frying

Small pinch sugar

1. Mix together the chili, turmeric, amchoor, salt, and chickpea flour.

2. Add the okra and toss until well coated.

3. Heat the oil in a frying pan and fry the okra in batches until crisp and golden. You may need to separate the frying okra with a fork.

4. Serve hot with a slight sprinkling of sugar for a hint of sweetness.

Preparation time: 15 minutes   Cooking time: 15 minutes

Many kinds of flours are used in Indian cooking. Chief among these are chickpea (or gram) flour, rice flour, and wheat flour. Sometimes these are all combined to make pancakes and breads. This fragrant stew from central India is thickened with wheat flour. It is light and nutritious. Serve it with Minted Pulao (see page 122) or with bread rolls. You can add any firm vegetable you want.

SUBZION KA STEW

vegetable stew

1. Heat a heavy saucepan and drop in the coconut and garam masala. Stir for a minute, remove, and blend the mixture in a coffee grinder. Set aside.

2. Heat the oil. Add the onion and let it soften. Add the chilies and tomatoes. Stir.

3. Gently mix the vegetables into the sauce. Mix the flour with a little water to make a paste. Add this to the pan and cook for a minute.

4. Add the salt, sugar, and the coconut-spice powder, and stir to blend. Serve hot with chopped cilantro sprinkled on top.

Preparation time: 20 minutes   Cooking time: 20 minutes

2 tablespoons dry, unsweetened coconut

1 teaspoon garam masala

2 tablespoons sunflower oil

1 medium onion, chopped

2 green chilies, slit

2 red tomatoes, chopped

1¼ pounds mixed vegetables (carrots, potatoes, green beans, peas), cubed and boiled

1 tablespoon flour

Salt, to taste

½ teaspoon sugar

Handful of cilantro, chopped

In India, a thin version of lassi *is called buttermilk. It is a popular drink in the summer and is easy to make: just stir a heaped tablespoon of yogurt into ⅔ cup cool water. It is sometimes flavored with flower essences or seasoned with salt. This recipe is from the palm-fringed state of Kerala, where it is served as part of a sit-down feast.*

AVIAL

vegetables in "buttermilk"

1. In a blender, grind the coconut, chilies, and cumin seeds with a little water to a fine paste.

2. Add this paste to the cooked vegetables and heat for a few minutes to blend.

3. Pour in the "buttermilk," add the sugar and salt, and heat through.

4. This rather thin stew goes well with plain boiled rice and poppadums.

Preparation time: 25 minutes   Cooking time: 15 minutes

1¾ cups dry, unsweetened coconut

2 green chilies

¼ teaspoon cumin seeds

1¼ pounds mixed vegetables (potatoes, plantain, squash, yam), peeled, cubed, and steamed

⅔ cup "buttermilk" (see above)

1 teaspoon dark brown sugar

Salt, to taste

Indians love Mexican food, and this recipe, although traditional, is inspired by that cuisine in its presentation. Crisp, tangy, and simple to make, these potatoes make a wonderful accompaniment to rotis and chicken or meat. You can also serve them at teatime for an unusual but filling snack. Choose floury potatoes, such as Idaho, for this dish.

ALOO BHARVAN

stuffed potato skins

1. Cut each potato in half and scoop out the centers, leaving a thick ridge of flesh on the skin.

2. Heat the oil in a large frying pan or deep-fat fryer and deep-fry the skins. Drain on paper towels.

3. Dust the skins with ground cumin and salt.

4. Mix the honey yogurt with chili powder and salt, and fill the fried skins.

5. Serve at once, garnished with the cilantro.

4 large unpeeled potatoes, boiled

Sunflower oil for deep-frying

1 teaspoon roasted ground cumin

Salt, to taste

6 tablespoons thick, whole-milk yogurt with 1 teaspoon honey

¼ teaspoon chili powder

Cilantro, for garnish

Preparation time: 10 minutes   Cooking time: 10 minutes

Broccoli is a new addition to Indian cooking, but its taste is ideally suited to lightly spiced stir-fries. Here it is flavored with ground coriander, which is made from the seeds of the coriander plant and tastes quite different from the leaves (which are called cilantro). The seeds are considered cooling and are added to many summer drinks. Serve this dish with a roti and Dudhi and Mint Raita (see page 27).

BROCCOLI KAJU KI SUBZI

broccoli with cashew nuts

1. Heat the butter or ghee and add the cumin seeds. As they pop, add the ground coriander and ginger-garlic paste. Fry for a few seconds only.

2. Add the broccoli, cashews, and salt. Stir and cook, adding a few teaspoons of water, until broccoli just softens.

3. Serve hot, drizzled with cream and fine strips of ginger, if you like.

Preparation time: 10 minutes   **Cooking time:** 15 minutes

Pat of butter or ghee

1 teaspoon cumin seeds

2 teaspoons ground coriander

1 teaspoon ginger-garlic paste

1¼ pounds broccoli florets

Handful of roasted cashews (if salted, just wash and dry first)

Salt, to taste

⅔ cup light cream

Fine strips of fresh ginger (optional)

The first sacrament in a Hindu's life is the naming ceremony, which is celebrated soon after birth. The baby's horoscope is cast, a name chosen, and great feasting follows. The Sindhi community that emigrated to India from the region of Sind, now in Pakistan, produce endless versions of this festive curry at such celebrations. It is served with rice and crisp fried potatoes. Cluster beans are a type of long bean sold in Indian food stores as guvar, but you can use green beans.

SINDHI KADHI

vegetable and tomato curry

1. Heat the oil in a large pan, add the fenugreek seeds and curry leaves. Let them darken. Add the ginger paste, and stir.

2. Add the vegetables and pour in 3 cups boiling water.

3. Mix the chickpea flour, tomato paste, and tamarind with a little water to make a paste. Add this to the pan. Add salt.

4. Cook until the vegetables are tender and the curry has thickened slightly.

5. Serve hot with finely shredded ginger on top, if you like.

Preparation time: 15 minutes   Cooking time: 15 minutes

2 tablespoons sunflower oil

½ teaspoon fenugreek seeds

A few curry leaves

1 teaspoon ginger paste

1¼ pounds (4–5 cups) mixed vegetables (eggplants, carrots, cluster beans or green beans, potatoes) cut into even-size pieces

1 tablespoon chickpea flour, roasted (see page 90, Cabbage and Green Pepper Stir-fry)

2 tablespoons tomato paste

1 teaspoon tamarind paste

Salt, to taste

Finely shredded fresh ginger (optional)

LENTILS, ALONG WITH RICE AND ROTIS, ARE STAPLE FOODS IN INDIA'S DIET. LENTILS ARE CALLED DAL, AND *DAL-ROTI* IS A HINDI TERM THAT REFERS TO EVERYDAY FOOD THAT IS COOKED IN THE HOME. A modern Indian meal at home usually consists of rotis or rice, a vegetable dish, and a dal (lentil) or other curry, with maybe a salad on the side.

Each region of India has its own ways of cooking lentils, beans, and seeds. In the south, they are flavored with fenugreek seeds and curry leaves; in the west, with jaggery (palm sugar) and tamarind; in the east, with anise and onion seeds; and in the north, with fried onions, tomatoes, and garlic. Kashmir has the best rajma or red kidney beans, which are cooked with only a few spices and served with sparkling white rice. In the south, black-eyed peas are combined with tamarind and coconut to make a tangy curry.

In days gone by, beans were mostly dried to increase their shelf life. Today, all kinds of precooked beans that do not require long soaking and simmering are available in cans. Sprouted beans are easier to digest and have a better vitamin C content than unsprouted ones.

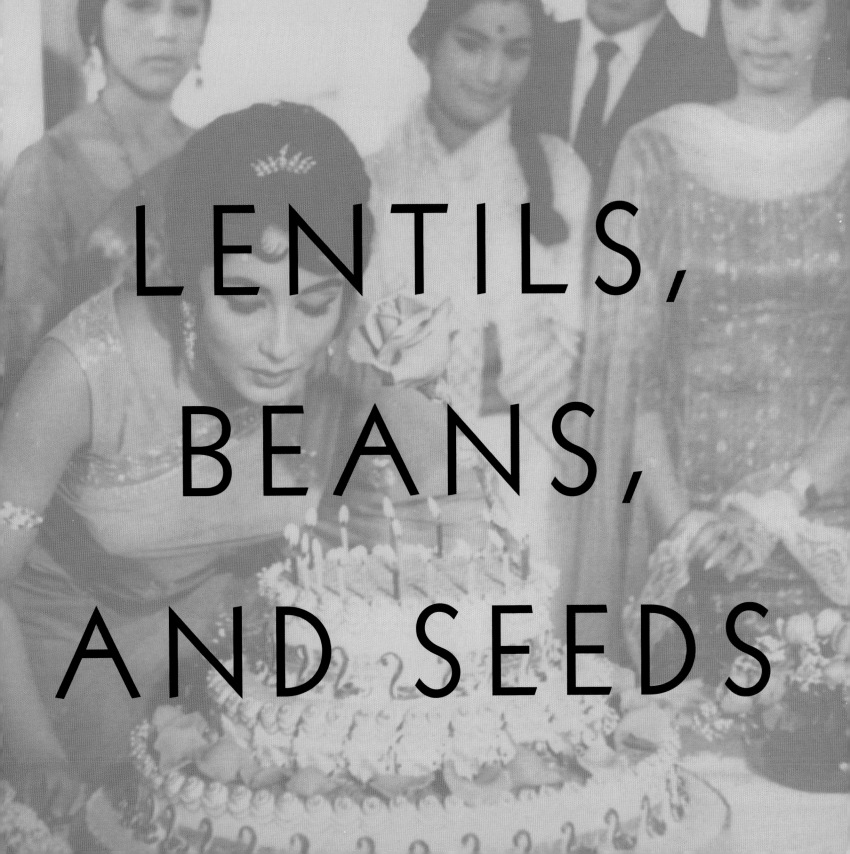

LENTILS, BEANS, AND SEEDS

Navratri is a nine-day festival in the autumn, about a month before Diwali. It celebrates the victory of the valiant goddess Durga, who fought evil for nine days and nine nights during this time. The people of Gujarat celebrate this vibrant festival by dancing the raas, a folk dance from the area, and by feasting on delicious vegetarian food. This is one dish prepared for the festival, and its sweet-and-sour flavor beautifully complements plain boiled rice. The peanuts create an exciting contrast of texture.

DANEDAR DAL
lentils with peanuts

1. Pour enough boiling water over the mung beans to cover them. Cook, adding more water, if necessary, until soft and mushy. Add more hot water to obtain a thin pouring consistency. Set aside.

2. In a wok, heat the oil and add the mustard seeds. As they begin to pop, add the curry leaves and the chili.

3. Stir in the tamarind pulp, turmeric, sugar, and a little water, and bring to a boil.

4. Add salt and the peanuts, let simmer for 2 minutes, and serve hot, sprinkled with cilantro.

Preparation time: 10 minutes   Cooking time: 15 minutes

1⅔ cups yellow split mung beans

2 tablespoons sunflower oil

½ teaspoon mustard seeds

6 curry leaves

1 fresh green chili, slit down the middle

2 tablespoons tamarind pulp

¼ teaspoon turmeric

3 teaspoons dark brown sugar

Salt, to taste

2 tablespoons salted peanuts

Handful of cilantro, chopped

This wonderful recipe is inspired by the cooking of the Zoroastrians, who came to India from Iran hundreds of years ago. It is served at festive occasions with Caramel-Flavored Rice (see page 124), a sweet carrot pickle, potato chips, and onion rings. Sometimes lamb or chicken is added while cooking. The white-skinned variety of squash is not a substitute for the orange here.

DHANSAK DAL

lentil and vegetable purée

1. Put the onion, squash, fenugreek, mint, eggplant, ginger-garlic paste, and lentils in a pan, cover with boiling water, and cook until mushy. Blend with a hand whisk.

2. Heat the oil and add the cumin seeds. When they pop, add the garam masala, tomato paste, and vinegar. Stir to blend.

3. Pour in the lentils, add salt, and serve hot, garnished with the cilantro.

Preparation time: 20 minutes   Cooking time: 20 minutes

1 large onion, chopped

2 tablespoons chopped squash (or canned squash purée)

2 tablespoons dried fenugreek leaves

2 tablespoons chopped fresh mint leaves

1 small eggplant, chopped

1 teaspoon ginger-garlic paste

5 ounces (a scant cup) split yellow lentils

2 tablespoons sunflower oil

1 teaspoon cumin seeds

1 teaspoon garam masala

1 tablespoon tomato paste

¼ cup distilled vinegar

Salt, to taste

Chopped cilantro, for garnish

This is one of the most popular dishes of Indian cooking and is served in almost every Indian restaurant anywhere in the world. I have sometimes made this in a hurry with a can of lentil soup. No one has been able to tell the difference! Here I give the longer version. Serve with rice or roti.

TARKA DAL

lentils with onion and garlic

1. Pour boiling water over the lentils and cook over low heat for 15 minutes.

2. Meanwhile, heat the oil in a pan and add the cumin seeds.

3. As the seeds begin to pop, add the onion and stir until golden and slightly crisp. Remove half the onion with a slotted spoon and drain on paper towels.

4. Add the tomato paste, ginger-garlic paste, chilies, and salt to the pan and cook until blended.

5. Carefully add the cooked lentils and adjust seasoning.

6. Serve hot, with reserved fried onions piled on top and a sprinkling of cilantro.

10 ounces (1⅔ cups) red split lentils

2 tablespoons sunflower oil

1 teaspoon cumin seeds

1 large onion, sliced

1 tablespoon tomato paste

1 teaspoon ginger-garlic paste

2 green chilies, slit

Salt, to taste

Handful of cilantro, chopped

Preparation time: 15 minutes   Cooking time: 15 minutes

Indian astrology links black-eyed peas with the planet Venus, hence in many parts of the country they are considered to be aphrodisiacs. In this southern India recipe, their buttery texture is combined with the smoothness of coconut milk and cream.

CHAWLI BENDI

black-eyed peas in coconut cream

1. Heat 1 tablespoon of oil in a saucepan and add the chilies, then the tamarind and garlic. Fry for 1 minute and grind to a fine paste in a coffee grinder or small blender.

2. Heat the remaining oil and fry this paste again, for 1 minute.

3. Add the coconut milk, beans, and salt. Heat through and serve.

3 tablespoons sunflower oil

4 dried red chilies, seeded

1 teaspoon tamarind paste

2 cloves garlic

1¼ cups coconut milk

One 15-ounce can black-eyed peas, drained and rinsed

Salt, to taste

Preparation time: 5 minutes   Cooking time: 10 minutes

CHOLE PANJIM

chickpeas in blazing red coconut curry

1. Heat 1 tablespoon oil in a frying pan and fry the ginger-garlic paste. Add the red chilies and let darken.

2. Add the coconut and stir until golden. Remove from the heat and stir in the garam masala.

3. Grind this mixture in a blender, along with some water, to make a fine paste.

4. Heat the remaining oil and fry the onion. Add the chickpeas and salt. Stir and add the red paste.

Stir, add enough water to make a sauce, and heat through. Serve hot.

Preparation time: 15 minutes   Cooking time: 10 minutes

3 tablespoons sunflower oil

1 teaspoon ginger-garlic paste

6 dried, very red chilies, seeded

5 tablespoons dry, unsweetened coconut

1 teaspoon garam masala

1 large onion, chopped

One 15-ounce can chickpeas, drained and rinsed

Salt, to taste

MILI JULI BEANS TAMATER

cannellini beans with tomatoes

1. Heat the oil in a frying pan and add the onion. Stir until translucent.

2. Add the garlic paste, turmeric, and chili.

3. Tip in the tomatoes and cook until well blended.

4. Add the beans, season with salt, and stir.

5. Pour in the cream, heat gently, and serve.

Preparation time: 10 minutes   Cooking time: 10 minutes

2 tablespoons sunflower oil

1 large onion, chopped

½ teaspoon garlic paste

½ teaspoon turmeric

½ teaspoon chili powder

1 cup canned chopped tomatoes

One 15-ounce can cannellini beans, drained and rinsed

Salt, to taste

⅔ cup light cream

This sharp curry is from southern India, where it is served as a soup or over steamed rice. It is flavored with whole cloves of garlic. In the villages, people hang strings of garlic outside their homes to ward off evil forces. This dish is often recommended to those whose appetite needs a boost.

JEER MEERYA KADHI

cumin and pepper curry

1. Heat half the oil, and lightly fry the cumin seeds and peppercorns.

2. Add the tamarind, coconut, and asafetida. Stir.

3. Grind this mixture, along with a little water, in a blender to make a smooth paste. Add 3 cups water to make a thin curry. Add salt and heat.

4. Heat the remaining oil. Add the garlic, brown it, and pour into the curry. Stir and serve hot.

2 tablespoons sunflower oil

1 teaspoon cumin seeds

10 peppercorns

1 teaspoon tamarind paste

10 ounces (3½ cups) dry, unsweetened coconut

Pinch asafetida

Salt, to taste

2 cloves garlic, lightly smashed

Preparation time: 10 minutes   Cooking time: 10 minutes

BEANS TIKKI

potato cakes topped with red beans

1. Combine the mashed potatoes, salt, and bread, and knead together. Shape into thick flat patties.

2. Heat the oil and shallow-fry the potato cakes, turning over until both sides are golden and crisp. Remove from the heat and keep warm.

3. To make the sauce, heat the oil and add most of the onion, reserving the rest for a garnish. Cook until softened.

4. Add the ginger-garlic paste, tomato paste, and spices, and stir to blend.

5. Add in the beans and salt, pour in 1¼ cups boiling water, and cook for a few minutes.

6. Serve the potato cakes topped with beans and sprinkled with the reserved onion. A little chopped cilantro adds fragrance. Serve any remaining bean sauce alongside.

Preparation time: 15 minutes   Cooking time: 15 minutes

4 large potatoes, boiled, peeled, and mashed
Salt, to taste
2 slices bread, soaked in water and squeezed
Oil for frying

FOR THE BEAN SAUCE
2 tablespoons sunflower oil
1 large onion, chopped
1 teaspoon ginger-garlic paste
2 tablespoons tomato paste
½ teaspoon turmeric
½ teaspoon chili powder
One 15-ounce can red beans,
    drained and rinsed
Salt, to taste
Chopped cilantro, for garnish (optional)

THE COMMERCIAL DISTRICT OF ANY INDIAN CITY HAS A WIDE CHOICE OF QUICK MEALS AVAILABLE ON LITTLE CARTS LINING THE STREET. EACH CART IS EQUIPPED WITH A STOVE TO FINISH THE COOKING IN FRONT OF YOU. One of the popular meals is Anda Bhurji—spicy scrambled eggs. A huge wok, or *kadhai,* sits on the stove into which the cook tosses a variety of herbs and spices, onions, garlic, and tomatoes, and a few spoonfuls of beaten egg. A brisk stir, a wild flourish with the *kadhai,* and the delicious meal is ready.

Eggs are incredibly versatile and all over India they are fried, scrambled, or cooked in curries with spices and herbs. Egg dishes are often associated with the cuisine of the Zoroastrians, the community that immigrated to India from Iran many centuries ago. Their food has become a unique blend of Indian and Iranian, and eggs are a prominent feature. Vegetables such as okra and potatoes are topped with a fried egg, or sweet semolina pudding is served garnished with a slice of boiled egg. Sunday breakfast can often be an omelette flavored with cumin, onion, and green chilies, served with ketchup and a buttered roll.

EGGS

Scrambled eggs are an international favorite. In India, this spiced version is served on toast for breakfast or with rotis or nans as a main meal. In the south, it is made with coconut milk for a creamier texture, and then flavored with green peppercorns.

AKOORI

parsi-style scrambled eggs

1. Beat the eggs with the salt and pepper.

2. Heat the oil in a frying or omelette pan, add the onion, and let soften.

3. Add the ginger-garlic paste, chilies, and cilantro. Stir for a minute, and add the ketchup.

Blend, and lower the heat.

4. Add the beaten eggs, stirring continuously until they firm up but remain spongy.

5. Serve hot.

6 large eggs

Salt and pepper, to taste

2 tablespoons sunflower oil

1 large onion, chopped finely

1 teaspoon ginger-garlic paste

¼ teaspoon green chilies, chopped

Handful of cilantro, chopped

1 tablespoon ketchup

Preparation time: 10 minutes   Cooking time: 10 minutes

MASALA AMLATE

pepper and chili omelette

1. Heat the oil in a frying pan and fry the ground pepper for a few seconds.

2. Add the green chilies. Pour in the eggs and cook, covered, over low heat until set into an omelette.

3. Sprinkle with the cheese and cilantro, and serve at once.

Preparation time: 10 minutes   Cooking time: 10 minutes

1 tablespoon sunflower oil

3 turns of the peppermill

2 green chilies, chopped

6 large eggs, beaten with salt and pepper

3 tablespoons grated cheddar cheese

Handful of cilantro, chopped

ANDE KE BHAJIA

egg fritters

1. Combine the flour, ajowan, chili, turmeric, and salt. Pour in just enough water to make a thick batter.

2. Heat the oil in a wok. Dip the egg halves individually in the batter. Fry until golden. Serve hot, garnished with a sprig of cilantro, if you like.

Preparation time: 10 minutes   Cooking time: 10 minutes

3 tablespoons chickpea flour

½ teaspoon ajowan seeds (ajwain)

½ teaspoon chili powder

½ teaspoon turmeric

Salt, to taste

Sunflower oil for deep-frying

4 large eggs, hard-boiled, peeled, and cut in half

Cilantro sprigs, chopped (optional)

This has to be one of the simplest and most delicious curries ever. Tiny Muslim eateries serve many versions of it with fat bread rolls and an onion salad. The addition of milk or cream, if you want to be indulgent, at the end is what brings all the ingredients together in a burst of flavor and taste. I serve this curry with hot nans, brushed with butter, and Sweet and Sour Potatoes Tossed in Spices (see page 34).

BAIDA CURRY

simple egg curry

1. Heat the oil in a large pan and add the cumin seeds. As soon as they darken, add the onion and cook to soften.

2. Add the ginger-garlic paste and tomato paste, and stir. Add the spices and salt. Blend until mushy.

3. Gently place the eggs in the curry and pour the milk or cream over them. Heat through and serve, sprinkled with cilantro.

Preparation time: 15 minutes   Cooking time: 10 minutes

2 tablespoons sunflower oil

½ tablespoon cumin seeds

2 large onions, chopped

1 tablespoon ginger-garlic paste

2 tablespoons tomato paste

½ teaspoon turmeric

½ teaspoon chili powder

1 teaspoon garam masala

Salt, to taste

8 large eggs, hard-boiled, peeled, and cut in half

3 tablespoons milk or cream

Handful of cilantro, chopped

This classic recipe comes from the kitchens of the Mughal kings who ruled Delhi for many centuries. Today it is made as part of a Muslim wedding feast along with biryani and desserts made with clotted milk and decorated with rose petals. This is a pretty-looking dish that adds glamour to a buffet. It can be served with a salad and french fries, as a light lunch.

NARGISI KOFTA

eggs encased in meat

1. Put the ground lamb, ginger-garlic paste, garam masala, lentils, salt, and chili in a pan. Add ⅔ cup water and cook until the meat and lentils are done, adding more water if necessary. Let all the water dry up. Remove from the heat and let cool.

2. Grind this mixture in a blender until fairly smooth. Stir in the beaten egg.

3. Completely coat each boiled egg with this mixture.

4. Heat the oil and, once it's hot enough, gently lower in each coated egg.

5. Fry until golden, then remove using a slotted spoon. Cut each fried egg *kofta* in half with a sharp knife, and serve hot with ketchup.

1¼ pounds lean ground lamb
2 teaspoons ginger-garlic paste
2 teaspoons garam masala
3 tablespoons yellow gram lentils
Salt, to taste
1 teaspoon chili powder
1 large egg, beaten
4 eggs, hard-boiled and peeled
Oil for deep-frying
Ketchup

Preparation time: 15 minutes   **Cooking time:** 35 minutes

TARKA BAIDA

indian-style fried eggs

1. Heat the oil and fry the cumin seeds.

2. Sprinkle in the turmeric and chili powder.

3. Break the eggs into the pan and lightly stir to break up the yolks.

4. As the eggs set, season with salt and pepper, and turn them over to cook the other side. Serve hot.

Cooking time: 5 minutes

FOR EACH SERVING
1 tablespoon sunflower oil
Pinch cumin seeds
Pinch turmeric
Pinch chili powder
2 large eggs
Salt and pepper, to taste

SAUCE KA ANDA

eggs in white sauce on toast

1. Melt the butter, add the flour, and stir. Whisk in the milk and blend until smooth and thick.

2. Add the chopped eggs, salt, and pepper, and stir lightly.

3. Serve on buttered toast with a sprinkling of chili powder and sprigs of cilantro.

Preparation time: 5 minutes   Cooking time: 5 minutes

Pat of butter
2 tablespoons flour
1¼ cups milk
6 eggs, hard-boiled, peeled, and
   chopped
Salt and pepper, to taste
4 slices wheat bread, toasted and
   buttered
Pinch chili powder
Cilantro sprigs, for garnish

BHARE ANDE

eggs stuffed with apricot rice

1. Heat the oil and toss in the apricots for 1 minute.

2. Add the rice and salt, and blend. Remove from the heat and stir in 1 tablespoon crème fraîche.

3. Fill the hollow of each egg half with this mixture.

4. Fold the yolks, remaining crème fraîche, and a little salt together, and pipe around each filled egg half. Serve garnished with cilantro.

Preparation time: 10 minutes   Cooking time: 10 minutes

1 tablespoon sunflower oil

1½ tablespoons chopped apricots

1 tablespoon cooked rice

Salt, to taste

3 tablespoons crème fraîche or, if unavailable, sour cream

4 eggs, hard-boiled, peeled, cut in half, yolks removed and set aside

Cilantro sprigs, for garnish

BAIDA MAKHANI

eggs in butter tomato sauce

1. Melt the butter and fry the ginger-garlic paste for a couple of minutes. Add the bay leaf.

2. Tip in the ground almonds and fry briefly. Add the tomato paste, spices, and salt. Stir to blend, adding ⅔ cup boiling water.

3. When the sauce bubbles, reduce the heat and place the eggs in the pan. Heat through.

4. Serve swirled with cream and a sprinkling of cilantro.

Preparation time: 15 minutes   Cooking time: 15 minutes

4 tablespoons butter

1 teaspoon ginger-garlic paste

1 bay leaf

¼ cup ground almonds

¼ cup tomato paste

½ teaspoon chili powder

½ teaspoon garam masala

Salt, to taste

4 eggs, hard-boiled, shelled, and cut in half

¼ cup heavy cream

Handful of cilantro leaves, chopped

This creamy curry is reminiscent of lazy days beside the azure lagoons of Kerala. The cuisine of this state, situated on the Malabar coast, is rich in coconut, which grows in abundance everywhere. The food is flavored with coconut oil but the taste can be a bit overpowering for the uninitiated. Serve this with rice and a poppadum. I sometimes add a few cherry tomatoes to the curry for color.

BAIDA MALABAR

eggs in coconut curry

1. Heat a pan and dry-roast the coriander seeds, cloves, and cardamom seeds until they darken. Add the coconut, and brown. Let the mixture cool slightly, then grind with a little water to a fine paste in a blender.

2. Heat the oil and add mustard seeds. As they pop, add the curry leaves, chili powder, salt, then the coconut mixture. Pour in the coconut milk.

3. Bring to a gentle boil. Place the eggs in the curry and finish with a couple of twists from a peppermill over the top, if you like.

Preparation time: 10 minutes   Cooking time: 20 minutes

1 tablespoon coriander seeds

4 cloves

½ teaspoon cardamom seeds

¼ cup dry, unsweetened coconut

3 tablespoons coconut oil (or sunflower, if you prefer)

1 teaspoon mustard seeds

10 curry leaves

½ teaspoon chili powder

Salt, to taste

1¼ cups coconut milk

4 eggs, hard-boiled, peeled, cut in half

INDIA'S EMERALD-GREEN RICE FIELDS ARE RESPLENDENT WITH MANY VARIETIES OF RICE. ALONG WITH WHEAT AND LENTILS, RICE IS PART OF THE STAPLE DIET OF ALL INDIANS. It is the symbol of prosperity, and many auspicious rituals are linked to it. Rice features in many festival menus, in sweet or savory forms. Festive pulaos and biryanis are always made with deliciously fragrant basmati—the undisputed king of rice.

Southern Indians are great lovers of rice and eat it at each meal with a variety of lentil curries. To finish, they mix it with thick, cool yogurt, and enjoy it spiced with a hot mango pickle. The north favors wheat. Punjab is called the granary of India because of its lush wheat fields. Many Indians buy whole wheat, clean it, and take it to the local *chakki,* or mill, to be ground into flour. However, nowadays, store-bought flour is also widely available and used by modern cooks. Sometimes rice or wheat noodles, called seviyan, are served with curries instead of rice, especially in the south. There are also innumerable crêpes, or dosas, that offer variety in taste and texture. These are stuffed or flavored and served with a coconut chutney and a spicy lentil curry called sambhar.

RICE
AND
BREADS

This is a popular and festive dish from Bombay. It is served at celebrations, such as weddings, and at events of ritual worship, where it is often enriched with nuts or dry fruit and served with a cool yogurt raita, *such as Dudhi and Mint Raita (see page 27), and a vegetable curry. On other days throughout the year it is combined with a rich meat curry, such as Caramelized Lamb and Potato Curry (see page 76).*

VANGI BHAAT

eggplant pulao

1. Heat the oil in a large frying pan and add the onion. Stir until it turns golden.

2. Add the washed rice and stir until it becomes opaque, then add the eggplant, turmeric, chili, garam masala, and salt and stir.

3. Add 2½ cups boiling water. Bring to a boil, then reduce the heat and cook, partly covered, until the rice is fluffy and tender (15–20 minutes). Add the lemon juice. Run a fork through the rice to loosen it, and serve hot.

Preparation time: 5 minutes   Cooking time: 25 minutes

2 tablespoons sunflower oil

1 medium onion, sliced

1¼ cups basmati rice, washed and drained

5 ounces eggplant, cut into 1-inch pieces

1 teaspoon turmeric

1 teaspoon chili powder

1 tablespoon garam masala

Salt, to taste

2 teaspoons lemon juice

RANGATDAR BHAAT
colorful vegetable pulao

1. Heat the oil in a large frying pan and fry the cumin seeds until they darken. Drop in the bay leaf.

2. Add the turmeric and the vegetables and mix.

3. Add the rice and salt. Stir. Pour in 2½ cups boiling water. Bring to a boil, then reduce the heat and cook, partly covered, until the rice is fluffy and tender (15–20 minutes).

4. Run a fork through the rice to loosen it and serve hot.

Preparation time: 15 minutes   Cooking time: 20 to 25 minutes

¼ cup sunflower oil

1 teaspoon cumin seeds

1 bay leaf

Pinch turmeric

5 ounces (1–1½ cups) prepared mixed vegetables (diced red peppers, mushrooms, carrots, and peas)

1¼ cups basmati rice, washed and drained

MURGH PULAO
chicken pulao

1. Place the chicken, garlic-ginger paste, garam masala, bay leaves, and onion salt in a pan with 2½ cups water. Bring to a boil.

2. Heat the oil in a large frying pan or saucepan and add the rice. Stir until it changes color.

3. Pour the chicken and stock mixture into the rice. Cover, and cook until the chicken and rice are done (15–20 minutes).

4. Serve sprinkled with the nuts and raisins.

Preparation time: 10 minutes   Cooking time: 20 to 25 minutes

10 ounces boneless chicken breast, cut into chunks

2 teaspoons ginger-garlic paste

1 teaspoon garam masala

2 bay leaves

Onion salt, to taste

2 tablespoons sunflower oil

1¼ cups basmati rice, washed and drained

3 tablespoons mixed nuts and raisins

It is likely that the Mughal rulers of Delhi introduced mint into Indian cookery.
Many homemakers in India grow fresh mint on a sunny kitchen windowsill. The
herb is used in chutneys and meat dishes, especially in northern India. A few
sprigs, slightly bruised, are also used to flavor tea. In this recipe, basmati rice gets
a fresh flavor and color with the addition of mint.

PUDINA PULAO

minted pulao

1. Grind the mint with a little water to a smooth paste.

2. Heat the ghee or oil in a large frying pan and fry the cumin seeds until dark.

3. Add the rice and salt and fry for one minute. Add the puréed mint.

4. Pour in 2½ cups boiling water. Bring to a boil, then reduce the heat and cook, partly

covered, until the rice is fluffy and tender (15–20 minutes).

5. Run a fork through the rice to loosen it, and serve steaming hot with a sprig of mint on

top, if you like.

Large handful of mint leaves

2 tablespoons ghee or
sunflower oil

1 teaspoon cumin seeds

1¼ cups basamati rice, washed
and drained

Salt, to taste

Mint sprigs, for garnish
(optional)

Preparation time: 10 minutes   Cooking time: 20 to 25 minutes

Tomato ketchup is very popular all over India and often takes the place of the sweet chutney that is served with savory snacks. It is also added to chicken or meat dishes for extra flavor and is available in many forms with the addition of other flavorings such as garlic or chilies. Many enthusiastic cooks make their own ketchup at home and bottle enough for six months at a time. Here it is stirred into a rice pulao. Seafood lovers can combine this with Coastal Lobster Curry (see page 46) for a real treat.

JHINGA PULAO

shrimp pulao

1. Heat the oil in a large, heavy frying pan and fry the cumin seeds. As they darken, add the onion and let soften. Add the ginger-garlic paste and the chilies.

2. Add the shrimp and stir.

3. Tip in the rice and ground cilantro. Blend and add the ketchup, salt, and half the chopped cilantro. Mix.

4. Pour in 2½ cups boiling water. Bring to a boil, then reduce the heat and cook, partly covered, until the rice is fluffy and tender (15–20 minutes).

5. Run a fork through the rice to loosen it, and serve with the remaining cilantro sprinkled on top.

3 tablespoons sunflower oil

1 teaspoon cumin seeds

1 large onion, chopped finely

1 teaspoon ginger-garlic paste

2 green chilies, slit

5 ounces cooked, frozen shrimp

1¼ cups basmati rice, washed and drained

1 teaspoon ground cilantro

¼ cup ketchup

Salt, to taste

Handful of cilantro, chopped

Preparation time: 15 minutes   Cooking time: 25 minutes

This Parsi recipe is traditionally served with Lentil and Vegetable Purée (see page 102) and Lacy Cutlets (see page 77). The caramel does not sweeten the rice; instead, it adds a rich aroma and color. This meal is often accompanied by a sweet, sparkling fruit drink made of raspberries or oranges.

BROWN RICE

caramel-flavored rice

1. Heat the oil in a large frying pan and fry the onion slices. Stir constantly until evenly browned. Drain on paper towels.

2. In a separate pan, heat the sugar until it caramelizes. Pour in the oil used to fry the onion, and add the peppercorns and bay leaf.

3. Tip in the rice, add salt and half the fried onions. Mix well. Pour in 2½ cups boiling water, bring back to a boil, then reduce the heat and cook, partly covered, until the rice is fluffy and tender (15–20 minutes). Remove the bay leaf, run a fork through the rice to loosen it, and serve hot, sprinkled with the remaining fried onions.

3 tablespoons sunflower oil
1 large onion, sliced
1 tablespoon sugar
8 peppercorns
1 bay leaf
1¼ cups basmati rice, washed and drained
Salt, to taste

Preparation time: 10 minutes   Cooking time: 20 to 25 minutes

This recipe comes from a community of warriors from the city of Kolhapur in Maharashtra. Their cuisine is largely meat-based and includes fiery curries and meat fritters, served with a chutney made of crushed green chilies.

   The combination of rice and meat is common to many countries. This pulao is flavored with turmeric, which balances the taste of all the other ingredients. Serve this dish with Beet Raita (see page 37).

GOLI BHAAT

rice with meatballs

1. Combine the ingredients for the meatballs and grind in a blender until smooth.

2. Form into cherry-size balls. Heat the oil and deep-fry the meatballs. Drain, and keep warm.

3. Pour 3 tablespoons of the oil into a clean pan and fry the onion. Stir until golden, drain on paper towels, and set aside.

4. Add the cloves to the oil and then tip in the rice. Fry for 1 minute. Sprinkle with turmeric and salt.

5. Pour in 2½ cups boiling water. Bring to a boil, then reduce the heat and cook, partly covered, until the rice is fluffy and tender (15–20 minutes).

6. To serve, run a fork through the rice to loosen it, fold in the meatballs, and serve topped with the fried onions and cilantro.

Preparation time: 15 minutes   Cooking time: 25 minutes

FOR THE MEATBALLS
5 ounces lean ground lamb

2 slices bread, crusts removed, soaked in water, and squeezed

1 teaspoon ginger-garlic paste

1 green chile

Salt, to taste

Sunflower oil for deep-frying

1 medium onion, sliced

3 cloves

1¼ cups basmati rice, washed and drained

½ teaspoon turmeric

Salt, to taste

Handful of cilantro, chopped, for garnish

BESAN KA AMLATE

vegetarian "omelette"

1. Combine the onion, tomato paste, cilantro, cumin, chickpea flour, and salt. Mix well. Add the juice from the onion and enough water to make a batter of dropping consistency.

2. Heat a frying pan and dot with oil. Ladle in a spoonful of batter and flatten with the back of the spoon into a 5-inch-diameter disk.

3. After 2–3 minutes, lift the omelette, flip over, add a little oil to the pan, and cook on the other side. Both sides should be golden.

4. Continue to make omelettes until all the batter is used up.

1 small onion, grated (reserve juice)

1 teaspoon tomato paste

2 tablespoons cilantro, chopped

½ teaspoon ground cumin

7 ounces (1¾ cups) chickpea flour

Salt, to taste

Sunflower oil for dotting the pan

Preparation time: 10 minutes   Cooking time: 20 minutes

DHODAK cucumber pancakes (right)

1. Combine all the ingredients except the oil, and blend, adding a little water until you get a batter of dropping consistency.

2. Heat a frying pan and dot with a little oil. Ladle a spoonful of batter and flatten with the back of the spoon into a 4-inch-diameter disk. After 2–3 minutes, flip over and cook on the other side.

3. Do the same for the rest of the pancakes and serve hot with a spicy meat dish and a *raita*.

5 ounces (1 cup) coarse semolina

1¾ cups dry, unsweetened coconut

¾ to 1 cup cucumber, peeled and grated

1 tablespoon soft brown sugar

Salt, to taste

Sunflower oil to dot the pan

Preparation time: 10 minutes   Cooking time: 10 minutes

KELE KI PURI

banana-flavored fried bread (left)

1. Knead the flour, oil, water, and banana into a stiff dough. (You may need a little less or more water than the quantity given, depending on the quality of the flour.)

2. Divide the dough into equal-size balls the size of a large cherry. Smear your palms with oil and smooth each ball.

3. Heat the oil in a wok or a large, heavy frying pan. Roll each ball out into a flat disk, 1-inch in diameter, flouring the board as necessary.

4. Once the oil is very hot, gently place the disk into the hot oil, pressing it down with the back of a slotted spoon until puffy and golden. Turn it over and fry for 1 minute. It will puff up only if the oil is hot enough and the disk has been submerged.

5. Lift out with a slotted spoon and drain on paper towels.

6. Proceed similarly for all the fried bread, adjusting the heat so that it doesn't brown excessively.

10 ounces (2¼ cups) whole-wheat flour
1 tablespoon sunflower oil
⅔ cup warm water
1 medium, ripe banana, mashed
Sunflower oil for deep-frying

Preparation time: 15 minutes   Cooking time: 20 minutes

DAHI PURI

yogurt bread

Knead the flour, oil, and yogurt into a stiff dough, then proceed as for the recipe above.

10 ounces (2¼ cups) whole-wheat flour
1 tablespoon sunflower oil
½ cup plain yogurt

Preparation time: 15 minutes   Cooking time: 20 minutes

DESSERTS PROVIDE A REAL PLATFORM ON WHICH TO DISPLAY CULINARY AND CREATIVE SKILLS. IN ORDER TO MAKE AN IMPACT, THEY MUST BE STUNNINGLY PRESENTED AS WELL AS DELICIOUS TO EAT. This chapter shows how basic, store-bought ingredients can be "dressed up" to create stunning Indian confections that will delight your guests.

India has a great tradition of desserts. No meal is complete without a "pudding," which is often served along with the main course itself. Indian desserts are largely milk-based and often contain fruits and vegetables or various grains and flours. Ice creams and *kulfis* are national favorites. Lush, juicy watermelons, pineapples, chikoos (sapotas), guavas, and sweet limes fill the markets throughout the year. But all Indians look forward to the summer, an exceptionally hot time, if only because the mangoes begin to ripen. Every household buys dozens of this fragrant fruit to eat on its own or combined with cream, ice cream, coconut milk, or yogurt.

The misconception that Indian desserts are too sweet is fast disappearing, and lighter, healthier versions are now made in most Indian homes.

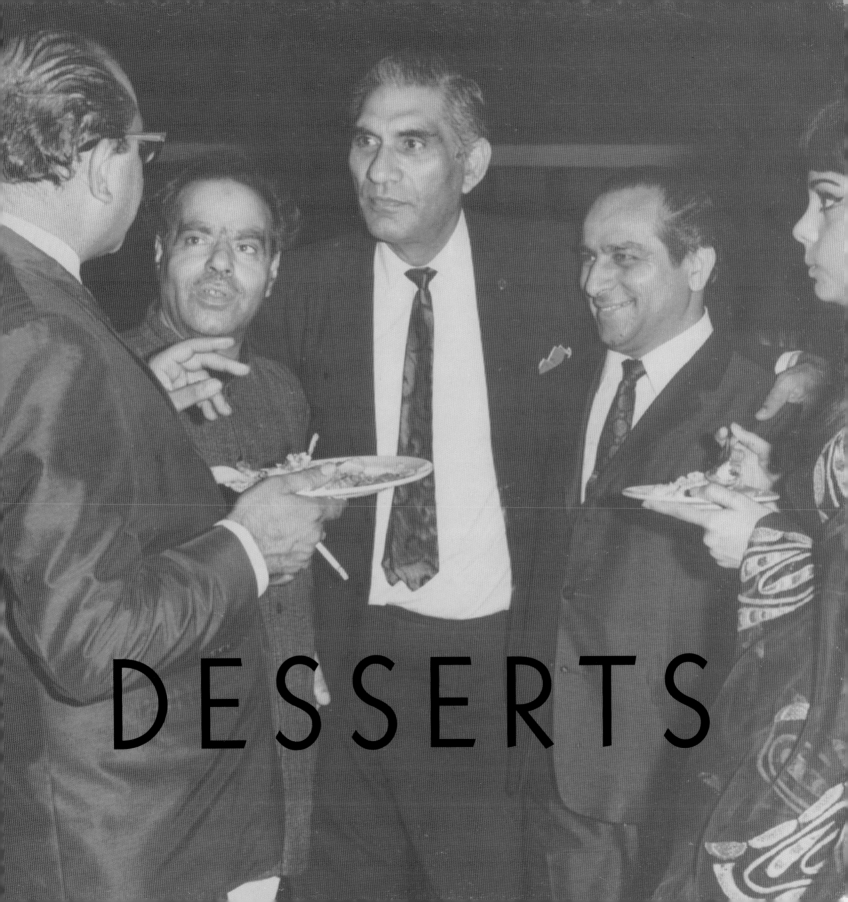

DESSERTS

PHALON KI BAHAR

mangoes and lychees with saffron cream   (right)

Mix together the yogurt, cream, sugar, saffron, milk, and cardamom, then add the mango and lychees. Serve chilled, decorated with fine slices of star fruit, if you like.

Preparation time: 20 minutes

½ cup thick, whole-milk yogurt
⅔ cup heavy cream
Sugar, to taste
½ teaspoon saffron strands, soaked in 1 teaspoon milk
Pinch ground cardamom
¾ to 1 cup mango, peeled and diced
¾ to 1 cup canned lychees, drained
Star fruit, for garnish (optional)

KHUBANI KA MEETHA

stewed apricots with cream

1. Put the apricots and sugar, along with 2½ cups water, in a heavy saucepan and cook until tender and pulpy.
2. Let cool, then spoon the mixture into individual serving glasses, sprinkle with almonds, drizzle the cream on top, and serve chilled.

Preparation time: 10 minutes   Cooking time: 15 minutes

10 ounces Hunza apricots, pitted
3½ ounces (½ cup) sugar
2 tablespoons crushed almonds
¼ cup heavy cream

The month of Ramadan is holy for Muslims the world over. Days of fasting end with nightly feasts after the moon has been sighted. People get together to break their fast with a variety of traditional dishes such as kabobs, biryanis, and flower-scented drinks. This creamy, rich dessert is served at such parties. It is typically set in little earthen pots and served with rose petals sprinkled on top.

PHIRNI

rose-flavored rice pudding

1. Mix the flour and a little of the milk to a paste.

2. Heat the rest of the milk with the sugar.

3. When very hot, add the paste, stirring constantly, until you get a custardlike consistency.
You may need a little more flour (depending on its quality).

4. Remove from the heat and stir in the essence. Pour into individual serving bowls and chill to set. This looks very pretty served sprinkled with rose petals.

3¼ ounces (¾ cup plus 2 tablespoons) rice flour

2½ cups milk

Sugar, to taste

Few drops rose essence

Preparation time: 5 minutes   Cooking time: 10 minutes + 1 hour setting time

SHUFTA
cottage cheese, nuts, and dried fruit in honey

1. Heat the ghee or butter and lightly fry the peppercorns and nuts.

2. Add the cardamom and sugar. Stir, and pour in ⅔ cup hot water. Drop in the saffron.

3. Bring to a boil and add the fruit and lemon juice. Cook until the syrup thickens.

4. Remove from the heat and add the paneer. Serve warm in individual bowls, with a small scoop of vanilla ice cream, if you like.

Preparation time: 10 minutes   Cooking time: 15 minutes

Pat of ghee or butter

4 peppercorns

3¼ ounces (½ cup) mixed nuts

3 cardamom pods, bruised

Sugar, to taste

Pinch saffron

¾ to 1 cup mixed dried fruit

1 teaspoon lemon juice

½ cup paneer (Indian cottage cheese), cubed

KELYACHE SHRIKHAND
banana in creamed yogurt

1. Combine the yogurt, crème fraîche, sugar, and cardamom, and beat until blended, which takes about 5 minutes.

2. Add the bananas and continue beating for 1 minute to mash them a little.

3. Spoon into serving glasses and top with the pistachios. Serve chilled.

Preparation time: 15 minutes

⅔ cup thick, whole-milk yogurt

⅔ cup crème fraîche, or, if unavailable, heavy or sour cream

Sugar, to taste

½ teaspoon ground cardamom

2 ripe bananas, sliced

1 tablespoon crushed pistachios

NARIAL KA HALWA

coconut pudding (right)

1. Heat a heavy pan and melt the sugar with a tablespoon of water. Add all the other ingredients and cook for 1 minute or so to blend everything together. Remove from the heat.

2. Serve hot, sprinkled over a scoop of vanilla ice cream, decorated with a slim lighted candle for effect.

Cooking time: 5 minutes

3¼ ounces (⅓ cup) granulated sugar

1¼ cups dry, unsweetened coconut

¼ teaspoon ground cardamom

Pinch saffron soaked in 1 teaspoon of milk

2 tablespoons pistachios, roughly crushed

ANANAS SHEERA

pineapple and semolina pudding

1. Melt the ghee or butter in a saucepan and fry the semolina until pink and fragrant. Reduce the heat and add the sugar. Let it melt.

2. Add the pineapple and stir. Pour in 1¼ cups hot water. Stir, and cook over a low heat, partly covered, until the semolina is cooked and the mixture is dry and fluffy.

Preparation time: 10 minutes   Cooking time: 15 minutes

5 ounces ghee or butter

5 ounces semolina (a heaping cup)

⅔ cup sugar

1 cup canned pineapple, drained and chopped

This is one of the few baked Indian sweets—almost like an Indian custard. It is delightfully rich and indulgent, yet it is simplicity itself to prepare. The silver foil creates a shimmery finale to the meal. The foil (varq) is sold in sheets in Indian food stores and has a shelf life of many years. (Silver foil is called chandi ka varq; *the gold is* sone ka varq.*)*

DOODH KA PUDDING

silver clotted milk cake

2½ cups evaporated milk
Sugar, to taste
4 medium eggs, beaten
½ teaspoon ground cardamom
1 sheet edible silver foil

1. Mix the milk and sugar and heat in a nonstick saucepan until the milk has reduced by a third. Take care not to burn the milk.

2. Let it cool completely, then fold in the eggs and cardamom.

3. Pour into a greased baking dish and bake in a water bath at 350°F until just set (this takes about 15 minutes).

4. Cool completely, then refrigerate. Serve decorated with silver foil.

Preparation time: 10 minutes   Cooking time: 40 minutes

SHAHI KHEER
crisp croutons in saffron milk

1. Heat the oil and fry the squares of bread until golden. Drain on paper towels.

2. Mix both milks and the saffron and bring to a boil. Simmer until it starts to become a little thick. Chill.

3. To serve, put a few fried bread croutons at the bottom of each serving dish, pour the saffron milk over them, and top with pistachios.

Sunflower oil for deep-frying

2 slices white bread (crusts on) cut into bite-size squares

1¼ cups evaporated milk

½ cup sweetened condensed milk, or to taste

Generous pinch saffron

2 tablespoons crushed pistachios

Preparation time: 10 minutes   Cooking time: 30 minutes

DUDHI HALWA
dudhi pudding

1. Melt the ghee or butter in a heavy pan, and fry the dudhi for a couple of minutes.

2. Add the milk and sugar and cook for 10–15 minutes or until the dudhi is pulpy.

3. Stir in the ground cardamom and remove from the heat.

4. Serve warm, with a scoop of vanilla ice cream, if you like.

2 tablespoons ghee or butter

1½ cups dudhi, peeled and grated

⅔ cup evaporated milk

3½ ounces (⅓ cup) sugar

¼ teaspoon ground cardamom

Preparation time: 10 minutes   Cooking time: 15 minutes

As summer approaches, a very special man may be seen on the streets of India. This is the ice-candy man, bringing a handcart lined with rows of bottles containing brightly colored syrups. This dessert is simple to make but involves the slightly tedious task of shaving or crushing the ice to wrap around a stick.

ICE GOLA

fruit-flavored ice-candy sticks (right)

1. Quickly mold the crushed ice around one end of a skewer to resemble a lollipop.

2. Sprinkle liberally with juice or syrup.

3. Present your ice-candy sticks, pierced into a melon, and eat quickly!

FOR EACH ICE CANDY

3 ice cubes, crushed

Various colored juices, syrups, or liqueurs (try rose, blue curaçao, etc.)

Wooden kabob sticks (skewers)

Preparation time: 15 minutes

AAMRAS

mango fool

1. Blend the mangoes to a smooth purée in a blender.

2. Add sugar, if necessary, and stir to dissolve.

3. Fold in the cream and the ground cardamom, and serve chilled.

1 pound ripe mangoes, peeled and sliced

Sugar, if needed

2 tablespoons heavy cream

½ teaspoon ground cardamom

Preparation time: 20 minutes

THE SCORCHING SUN AND RELENTLESS HEAT OF INDIA MAKE IT IMPERATIVE TO HAVE AN ELABORATE REPERTOIRE OF DRINKS. Water is, of course, the most preferred thirst-quencher and is always served with a meal. Fruit-based drinks are also popular. The most common is fresh lemonade, called nimboo pani, which is sold everywhere, including street stalls. Juices such as orange, pineapple, watermelon, and grape are sold at juice centers where you can park your car and order a quenching glass. These centers are found in every city and town of India. There are also floral essence–based drinks, including rose; *khus*, made from vetiver; and *kewra*, distilled from the screw pine flower. The yogurt drink, *lassi*, cools the body and aids digestion. It is served sweet or salted, at the beginning of a meal, to sip throughout, or at the end as a digestive.

India does not have a great alcohol tradition. When the Maharajas ruled, the imperial kitchens would prepare exclusive liqueurs to tempt the royal palate. These days, wine of good quality is produced, especially in the state of Maharashtra, around Bombay. However, one of the most sought-after liqueurs remains the Goan *feni*, made from the ripest, juiciest cashew fruit.

DRINKS

Just as there are juice centers all over India, there are milk bars, too, selling milk drinks, yogurt, lassi, and milk puddings. In the winter, when the weather is cool enough for the cultivation of berries, raspberry and strawberry milk is sold at these bars.

RASPBERRY KA DOODH

raspberry milkshake

1. Whiz everything together in a blender until smooth.

2. Chill, and serve in tall glasses.

Preparation time: 15 minutes

1 cup raspberries, hulled, washed, and drained

½ cup plain yogurt

1¼ cups milk

Honey, to taste

ADRAK CHAI

ginger tea

1. Bring the water to a boil and add the ginger.

2. Simmer for 1 minute and add the tea leaves.

3. Pour in the milk and bring to a boil. Remove from the heat, strain, and serve, with sugar, if you like.

Preparation time: 2 minutes   Cooking time: 10 minutes

2½ cups water

1-inch piece of fresh ginger, bruised

tea leaves to taste (depending upon the quality) about 2 to 3 heaping teaspoons

Milk and sugar, to taste

Indian tea is always served with milk and sugar. In Kashmir, a thick sweet brew called kahwa *is popular. In other parts of the country, you can choose from the teas of Assam or Darjeeling, or blended ones, for a fuller flavor. This recipe is a real pick-me-up and is wonderfully refreshing in the afternoon.*

MASALA CHAI
spiced tea

1. Put the water in a pan to boil along with the spices and the lemongrass.
2. Boil for 1 minute, then add the tea leaves and simmer over low heat for 1 minute.
3. Pour in the milk, heat through, strain, and serve, with sugar, if you like.

Preparation time: 5 minutes   Cooking time: 10 minutes

2½ cups water
Large pinch ground cardamom
2 cloves, bruised
½ teaspoon allspice
A few blades lemongrass
Tea leaves, to taste (about 2 to 3 heaping teaspoons)
Milk and sugar, to taste

PIYUSH
saffron-flavored "buttermilk"

Whisk everything except the nuts until smooth, chill, and serve in individual glasses, with the nuts on top.

Preparation time: 10 minutes

1 cup thick, whole-milk yogurt
Honey, to taste
Large pinch saffron dissolved in a little milk
1¼ cups cold water
2 tablespoons crushed pistachios

NIMBU KA SHARBAT

Indian lemonade

½ cup lemon juice
¼ cup sugar
1 teaspoon salt
½ teaspoon black pepper

Combine all the ingredients and add 2½ cups water. Drop in a few ice cubes and ser

in tall frosted glasses, with a slice of lime and a sprig of mint, if you like.

Preparation time: 10 minutes

left watermelon cooler, *right* Indian lemonade

KALINGAD KA SHARBAT

watermelon cooler

10 ounces (1¼–1½ cups) ripe
watermelon, cubed
¼ cup milk

Whiz the melon in a blender until smooth. Strain, add the milk, and serve chilled.

Preparation time: 10 minutes

This is a more festive version of salted lassi from the state of Maharashtra. It is usually served with all the herbs and spices left in it, but I like to strain it for a smoother drink. It is served with spicy meat and vegetable dishes or at the end of a meal as a digestive.

MATTHA

spiced lassi with cilantro

1. Grind the cilantro, chili, and cumin seeds finely in a blender, with a little water, until you have a coarse paste.

2. Combine this mixture with the water, yogurt, and coarse salt. Beat well. Strain through a fine strainer. Serve cold.

Preparation time: 10 minutes

Handful of cilantro

1 green chili

1 teaspoon cumin seeds, roasted

1¼ cups cold water

1 cup plain yogurt

Coarse or kosher salt, to taste

EVERY INDIAN MEAL IS ACCOMPANIED BY AN ASSORTMENT OF CHUTNEYS, RELISHES, AND PICKLES, BOTH SWEET AS WELL AS HOT, MANY OF THEM HOMEMADE. Pickles are made with a variety of seasonal fruits and vegetables such as lemons and limes, carrots, turnips, cauliflower, eggplants, figs, and apples. These are preserved in salt, spices, oil, vinegar, or lemon juice. Each state—and each community—has a particular recipe, depending on local ingredients. Goan prawn pickles or the chicken and lamb pickles from Punjab are famous throughout India. In Kerala, pickled peppercorns are found in every pantry, and Bengal loves its fish pickle in mustard oil. No pickle recipes are included here as they take a long time to prepare and need to be matured in bright, hot sunlight— guaranteed in India but perhaps not in other countries!

Chutneys and relishes add a sharp, pungent, or hot taste to a meal. They are prepared daily, as their shelf life is limited. (In India, we use the word *chutney* for relishes and dry or wet chutneys.) Chutneys involve grinding ingredients such as peanuts, coconut, cilantro, and garlic to a paste. Relishes are made by cooking diced ingredients in sugar, syrup, or vinegar.

CHUTNEYS
AND
RELISHES

This is surely the most popular Indian chutney of all. It is served with pancakes and bhajias, filled into sandwiches, and eaten with rice and dal. It does not keep very well and must be eaten fresh.

DHANIA CHUTNEY

green cilantro and peanut chutney

1. Grind everything in a blender with some water, to a fine paste.

2. Adjust seasoning and serve.

Preparation time: 10 minutes

Large handful of cilantro

2 tablespoons roasted peanuts

2 green chilies

1 teaspoon ginger-garlic paste

½ teaspoon sugar

Salt, to taste

1 tablespoon lemon juice

This recipe can be made and stored in the refrigerator for up to three days. Its sweet-and-sour taste complements anything from barbecued meats to rotis.

MANUKA TAMATER KI CHUTNEY

raisin and tomato relish

1. Heat the oil and drop in the mustard seeds. When they pop, add the cumin seeds and green chilies and stir.

2. Add the tomatoes, sugar, raisins, and salt, and cook until mushy. Cool and store in a jar.

Preparation time: 5 minutes   Cooking time: 10 minutes

2 tablespoons sunflower oil

½ teaspoon mustard seeds

½ teaspoon cumin seeds

2 green chilies, chopped

One 14½-ounce can peeled and chopped plum tomatoes

2 tablespoons sugar

2 tablespoons raisins

Salt, to taste

LAHSUN CHUTNEY
garlic and dried coconut chutney

1. Heat a pan and dry-roast the coconut until brown. Add the salt and the red chilies, and roast for another minute.

2. Remove from the heat, add the garlic and tamarind, and blend the entire mixture in a coffee grinder until fairly fine.

3. Store in a glass jar in the refrigerator.

Preparation time: 10 minutes

5 ounces dry, unsweetened coconut
Salt, to taste
5 dried red chilies
5 cloves garlic
½ teaspoon tamarind paste

NASHPATI CHUTNEY
pear chutney

Combine all the ingredients and cook until soft and pulpy. Use on the day it is prepared.

Preparation time: 10 minutes   Cooking time: 10 minutes

½ teaspoon anise, roasted and ground
Pinch nutmeg
3 large sweet pears, peeled and cubed
1½ tablespoons sugar
2 tablespoons lemon juice

DIWALI DINNER

As winter sets in, the most wonderful festival of lights, Diwali, is celebrated with great merriment and visual displays. During the five days of Diwali, families get together to celebrate the festival with fireworks, draw *rangolis,* or floor patterns, with chalk and rice flour outside their homes, and, of course, sweet and savory feasts. A mouth-watering feast and a variety of sweetmeats are prepared for family and friends to share. Boxes of dried fruits, nuts, and milk toffees, baskets of fruit, and tins of sweets made from milk, flour, and wheat are exchanged to ring in the Hindu New Year. By the end of the five-day festival, the merrymakers are so replete, it is hard to return to the daily routine.

MENU   Poories   kaju pulao

Amrood ka   Aloo muttar   Meethi mathri
sherbat   Vali ambat

AMROOD KA SHERBET

guava cooler

2 medium-ripe guavas, chopped
6 tablespoons sugar
1¼ cups water
1¼ cups milk

1. Combine the guavas, sugar, and water, and cook over high heat until the fruit becomes pulpy.
2. Strain through a fine-mesh strainer, pressing the mixture to collect as much fruit juice and purée as possible.
3. Let cool, then pour in the milk. Add more sugar according to taste. Serve cold.

Preparation time: 10 minutes   Cooking time: 10 minutes

POORIES

fried bread

1 pound (3¾ cups) whole-wheat flour
1 tablespoon sunflower oil
Warm water for kneading
Sunflower oil for deep-frying

1. Combine the flour and oil with your fingertips into a stiff dough, adding warm water as necessary, and knead until you have a smooth ball that leaves the sides of the bowl.
2. Heat the oil in a deep wok or *kadhai* until it is almost smoking. Divide the dough into large cherry-size balls.
3. Roll out each ball into a flat disk, flouring the board as necessary.
4. Carefully lower the disk into the hot oil using a slotted spoon. Submerge it, using the back of the spoon, and it should puff up.
5. Turn it over and fry until golden. Remove and drain on paper towels. Continue with the rest of the poories.

Preparation time: 15 minutes   Cooking time: 15 minutes

ALOO MUTTAR

pea and potato stir-fry

3 tablespoons sunflower oil
1 teaspoon cumin seeds
1 large green chili, slit
9 ounces (2¼ cups) frozen peas
½ teaspoon turmeric
1 teaspoon ground cilantro
Salt, to taste
Pinch of sugar
9 ounces (1¾–2 cups) baking potatoes, peeled, cubed and boiled
Handful of chopped cilantro
1 tablespoon lemon juice

1. Heat the oil in a large frying pan and fry the cumin seeds until they darken slightly.
2. Add the chili and the peas. Tip in the ground spices, salt, and sugar. Add a little water and cook until the peas are tender.
3. Add the potatoes; stir well to ensure they are heated through. Serve hot, sprinkled with chopped cilantro and lemon juice.

Preparation time: 5 minutes   Cooking time: 20 minutes

VALI AMBAT

beans in tangy coconut curry

This fragrant curry is wedding fare in southern India, where the meal is served on a banana leaf and rows of people sit together to eat. Professional serving staff, along with members of the bride's family, coax the guests to taste countless, tempting vegetarian dishes. This one is traditionally eaten with rice.

2 tablespoons sunflower oil
¼ teaspoon fenugreek seeds
4 dry red chilies
1 teaspoon tamarind paste
3 tablespoons dry, unsweetened coconut
½ teaspoon turmeric
One 14-ounce can mixed beans, drained and rinsed
Salt, to taste
Handful of chopped cilantro

1. Heat half the oil and fry the fenugreek seeds until they turn dark. Drop in the whole chilies and cook for 2 minutes.
2. Grind the fried spices, tamarind, coconut, turmeric, and a little water to a paste in a blender.
3. Heat the remaining oil and fry this paste for a minute. Add the beans and salt. Stir in enough hot water to obtain a pouring consistency.
4. Serve hot, sprinkled with cilantro.

Preparation time: 10 minutes   Cooking time: 10 minutes

KAJU PULAO

cashew pulao

Dried nuts and fruit are considered luxurious all over India. The best cashews come from Goa and Kerala, where they are fat, smooth, and shiny. Use whole cashew nuts in this recipe as they look so much prettier than broken ones.

3 tablespoons sunflower oil
6 peppercorns
3 cloves
Handful of cashews
1¼ cups basmati rice, washed and drained
2½ cups hot water
Salt, to taste

1. Heat the oil and fry the peppercorns and cloves for a minute. Add in the cashews and stir until they turn golden.
2. Tip in the rice and fry for a couple of minutes. Pour in the water, season with salt, and bring to a boil.
3. Reduce heat and simmer, partially covered, until the rice is done. Fluff up with a fork and serve hot.

Preparation time: 5 minutes   Cooking time: 20 minutes

MEETHI MATHRI

sweet crunchy cookies

1¼ cups flour
2 tablespoons semolina
1 tablespoon sunflower oil plus extra for deep-frying

FOR THE SYRUP
⅓ cup sugar
½ teaspoon ground cardamom
pinch of saffron
2 tablespoons crushed pistachios

1. Mix the flour, semolina, and a tablespoon of oil and knead into a stiff dough, adding water as necessary.
2. Heat the oil in a deep wok or *kadhai*. Divide the dough into 12 balls and roll out each one into a disk, about 2½ inches wide by a ¼ inch thick. Deep-fry, turning over the disks, until golden on both sides. Let cool.
3. To make the syrup, boil the sugar with ¼ cup water over high heat until slightly thick and sticky—about 15 minutes.
4. Tip in the cardamom and saffron. Dip each mathri into the syrup.
5. Sprinkle with nuts and arrange on a plate to cool. Serve with whipped cream or ice cream.

Preparation time: 15 minutes   Cooking time: 25 minutes

CHRISTMAS DINNER

Christmas is celebrated by Christians all over India as a festival of peace and forgiveness. Garlands of twinkling lights, Christmas trees, and lanterns in the shape of a star decorate each home. Many tree-lined avenues are lit up, and cardboard cutouts of Santa Claus and reindeer lure shoppers into department stores. The air is full of festive cheer even though there is neither snow nor cold winter breezes here. India enjoys a warm, tropical Christmas, and partygoers can be seen wearing skimpy, summery clothes!

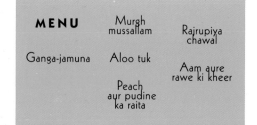

MENU

Murgh mussallam

Rajrupiya chawal

Ganga-jamuna

Aloo tuk

Aam aure rawe ki kheer

Peach aur pudine ka raita

GANGA-JAMUNA

fruit juice medley

1¼ cups orange juice
1¼ cups pineapple juice
½ teaspoon coarse or kosher salt
½ teaspoon roasted ground cumin

Combine all the ingredients and serve chilled with a sprig of mint, if you like.

Preparation time: 10 minutes

MURGH MUSSALLAM

whole roasted chicken with dried fruit and spices

One 3-pound corn-fed chicken

FOR THE MARINADE
⅔ cup plain yogurt
2 teaspoons ginger-garlic paste
Salt, to taste
3 tablespoons lemon juice
2 teaspoons chili powder
2 teaspoons garam masala

3 ounces (1 cup) dry, unsweetened coconut
3 ounces (1 cup) ground almond
3 tablespoons applesauce
¼ teaspoon saffron
Ghee for basting, or butter

1. Make cuts in the chicken. Combine the marinade ingredients and spread over the chicken. Marinate for at least 2 hours.

2. Blend the coconut, almond, applesauce, and saffron to a paste with a little water.
3. Smear the coconut mixture all over the chicken. Adjust seasoning. Place in a roasting tray, dot with ghee, and roast at 375°F until done. Baste occasionally to keep chicken from drying. Serve hot.

Preparation time: 15 minutes + 2 hours marinating
Cooking time: 45 minutes

ALOO TUK

crispy fried tangy potatoes

Sunflower oil for deep-frying
10 ounces (2–3 medium) potato wedges, skin on
Coarse or kosher salt, to taste
Generous pinch of chili powder
Generous pinch of roasted ground cumin
Generous pinch of mango powder (amchoor)

1. Heat the oil and fry the potato wedges until golden.

2. Sprinkle liberally with salt and spices, and serve hot.

Preparation time: 10 minutes Cooking time: 15 minutes

PEACH AUR PUDINE KA RAITA

peach and minty yogurt

A spicy meat dish is delicious when set off by a cool, fruity accompaniment. This combination of peach and mint is exotic and unusual. Peaches grow in the cool orchards of northern India and are sold all over the country. For this Christmas menu, I have used canned peaches. You could use fresh, ripe ones if making this in the summer.

1 small can peach slices, drained, juice reserved
⅔ cup plain yogurt
Salt, to taste
2 tablespoons chopped fresh mint leaves
½ teaspoon roasted ground cumin

Combine the peach slices, yogurt, salt, and mint leaves. Stir in 3 tablespoons of reserved peach juice and serve with a sprinkling of roasted ground cumin.

Preparation time: 10 minutes

RAJRUPIYA CHAWAL

gold and silver rice

India is a land of color and the national favorites are gold and silver. During all celebrations, traditional delicacies are served on carved silver platters. At weddings, the hall is decorated with gold, saffron, and crimson flowers, interlaced with green mango leaves.

2 tablespoons ghee (if unavailable, use butter)
½ teaspoon cumin seeds
A few mushrooms, sliced
1¼ cups basmati rice, washed and drained
½ teaspoon salt
1 teaspoon turmeric
2½ cups hot water
1 sheet edible silver foil (varq)

1. Heat the ghee in a heavy pan and fry the cumin seeds until they begin to darken.
2. Add the mushrooms. Tip in the rice, salt, and turmeric. Stir to blend.
3. Pour in the hot water, stir, and bring to a boil. Reduce heat and simmer, partially covered, until done.
4. Serve hot, decorated with a sheet of varq or edible silver foil.

Preparation time: 5 minutes Cooking time: 25 minutes

AAM AUR RAWE KI KHEER

warm semolina custard with mango

This simple recipe is the combination of two festive desserts. As fresh mangoes are not available at Christmas time, I use canned, sweetened pulp, called aamras, which is available in Indian shops and is perfectly acceptable. In fact, in India, canned or frozen mango pulp is often served at formal banquets when the fruit is out of season.

Pat of butter
5 tablespoons semolina
1¼ cups water
Sugar, to taste
1 cup coconut milk
Pinch of ground cardamon
½ cup canned mango pulp

1. Heat the butter and fry the semolina for a few minutes. Pour in the water and cook the semolina. Add the sugar.
2. Remove from the heat and stir in the coconut milk and the cardamom.
3. Pour into individual stemmed glasses and let set for a couple of minutes.
4. Top the custard with some mango purée and serve warm. This dessert tastes lovely cold, too.

Preparation time: 5 minutes Cooking time: 15 minutes

HOLI MENU

Around the time of the vernal equinox, the festival of Holi heralds the arrival of spring. It is celebrated by the lighting of bonfires that signify the destruction of evil and by throwing color on each other in a ritual of rejuvenation and joy. This custom celebrates the story of how the god Krishna played Holi with his friends, drenching them in colors made from wildflowers and fruit. Merrymakers drink an intoxicant called bhang and urge hesitant friends to join in the fun. This menu has all the colors to celebrate the spirit of Holi.

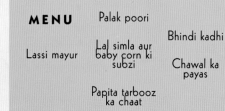

MENU
Palak poori
Lassi mayur
Lal simla aur baby corn ki subzi
Bhindi kadhi
Chawal ka payas
Papita tarbooz ka chaat

LASSI MAYUR

rainbow lassi

2¼ cups thick, whole-milk plain yogurt
6 tablespoons water
Sugar, to taste
2 teaspoons colored sugar, for garnish

1. Put the yogurt, water, and sugar into a blender and whiz until blended and frothy.
2. Pour into four glasses and gently place half a teaspoonful of colored sugar on top of each one. The lassi must be thick enough to hold the sugar on top.

Preparation time: 15 minutes

PALAK POORI

spinach bread

1 pound (3¾ cups) whole-wheat flour
1 tablespoon sunflower oil
¼ cup canned spinach purée
Pinch of salt
Warm water for kneading
Sunflower oil for deep-frying

1. Combine the flour, 1 tablespoon of oil, spinach purée, and salt. Pour in the water a little at a time and knead into a stiff dough.
2. Heat the oil in a *kadhai* or deep wok. Shape the dough into even-size balls.
3. Roll each ball into a flat disk on a floured board. Shake off excess flour and fry the disk, or poori, in the hot oil, submerging it with the back of a slotted spoon so that it puffs up. Turn it over and cook for a minute. Remove and drain on paper towels.
4. Proceed similarly for the rest of the poories. Serve hot.

Preparation time: 15 minutes   Cooking time: 20 minutes

LAL SIMLA AUR BABY CORN KI SUBZI

red pepper and baby corn

2 tablespoons sunflower oil
½ teaspoon cumin seeds
1 medium onion, sliced
2 tomatoes, quartered
½ teaspoon turmeric
½ teaspoon chili powder
10 ounces (1½ cups) red pepper, seeded and sliced
3½ ounces baby corn, each cut in half
Handful of cilantro, chopped

1. Heat the oil and add the cumin seeds. Let them darken. Add the onion and let it soften.
2. Add the tomatoes, spices, and salt, and cook until slightly pulpy.
3. Add the vegetables. Stir, cover, and cook until the peppers are just beginning to wilt. Serve sprinkled with cilantro.

Preparation time: 10 minutes   Cooking time: 15 minutes

PAPITA TAR-BOOZ KA CHAAT

papaya and melon salad

Both of these orange fruits bring fragrance and flavor to the table. Their color evokes the saffron powder that people throw on each other to celebrate the festival. This is made from bright orange kesariya flowers. Choose ripe fruit that is firm to the touch.

1 cup papaya, cubed
5 ounces (1 cup) pink melon, cubed
1 tablespoon lemon juice
Coarse or kosher salt, to taste
Handful of orange geranium flowers,
  for garnish (optional)

1. Gently combine the papaya, melon, lemon juice, and salt.
2. Serve sprinkled with the geranium flowers, if you like.

Preparation time: 15 minutes

BHINDI KADHI

okra in yogurt curry

Sunflower oil for deep-frying
5 ounces baby okra, with tops snipped off
Salt, to taste
2 tablespoons chickpea flour
1¼ cups plain yogurt
¼ cup sugar
½ teaspoon fenugreek seeds
6 cloves
Black peppercorns
10 curry leaves
3 dried red chilies

1. Heat the oil in a deep wok or *kadhai* and fry the okra until crisp. Drain on paper towels, sprinkle with salt, and set aside.
2. Whisk together the flour, yogurt, sugar, and salt, along with enough water to make a pouring consistency.
3. Cook this, stirring constantly until thick and creamy. Do not let the yogurt curdle. Simply whisk the sauce if this happens.
4. Heat 3 tablespoons oil in a small pan and add the fenugreek seeds, cloves, and peppercorns. Let them darken. Add the curry leaves and chilies and pour into the yogurt sauce.
5. Serve the sauce in a shallow dish with a heap of fried okra in the center.

Preparation time: 5 minutes   Cooking time: 25 minutes

CHAWAL KA PAYAS

rich rice pudding

This dessert is considered one of the most auspicious of all Indian sweets and is made at almost every feast all over the country. It is also offered to the gods as a "pure" food. Here I have added color to make it special for Holi. Choose any edible food color to make it look spectacular.

3½ ounces (½ cup) basmati rice, washed
  and drained
2½ cups milk
1¼ cups evaporated milk
¼ cup ground almond
Sugar, to taste
½ teaspoon ground cardamom
Edible food color, as needed

1. Bring the rice to a boil with the milk. Reduce heat and simmer until soft. Mash slightly with a whisk.
2. Pour in the evaporated milk, add ground almond and sugar, and heat through.
3. Remove from the heat and stir in the ground cardamom. Divide into four serving bowls and swirl a different shade of food color in each one. You can also layer the different colors in each bowl for a rainbow effect. Serve cold.

Preparation time: 15 minutes   Cooking time: 15 minutes

INDEX